nowhere but up

teen edition

"What can I say—I love Pattie Mallette! She is one of the strongest, bravest, and most caring people I know. Her story is riveting, but more than that, it's a testimony to the truth that God brings good out of even the darkest of times."

—**Judah Smith**, *New York Times* bestselling author of *Jesus Is* and lead pastor of The City Church

nowhere but up

teen edition

The Story of **Justin Bieber's** Mom

pattie mallette

WITH A. J. GREGORY

Revell

a division of Baker Publishing Group
Grand Rapids, Michigan

Published by Revell
a division of Baker Publishing Group
P.O. Box 6287, Grand Rapids, MI 49516-6287
www.revellbooks.com

Printed in the United States of America

Library of Congress Cataloging-in-Publication Data is on file at the Library of Congress, Washington, DC.

ISBN 978-0-8007-2200-5

Unless otherwise indicated, Scripture quotations are from the Holy Bible, New International Version®. NIV®. Copyright © 1973, 1978, 1984, 2011 by Biblica, Inc.™ Used by permission of Zondervan. All rights reserved worldwide. www.zondervan.com

Scripture quotations labeled NLT are from the *Holy Bible*, New Living Translation, copyright © 1996, 2004, 2007 by Tyndale House Foundation. Used by permission of Tyndale House Publishers, Inc., Carol Stream, Illinois 60188. All rights reserved.

Scripture quotations labeled *The Message* are from *The Message* by Eugene H. Peterson, copyright © 1993, 1994, 1995, 2000, 2001, 2002. Used by permission of NavPress Publishing Group. All rights reserved.

Lyrics in chapter 11 are from "Waves of Grace," written by David Noble. Copyright 1995. LITA Music (ASCAP). Administered by Justin Peters/Songs for the Planet, Inc., P.O. Box 40251, Nashville, TN 37204. International copyright secured. All rights reserved. Used by permission.

All dates, place names, titles, and events in this account are factual. The names of certain characters and some details have been changed in order to protect the privacy of those involved.

Life Projects is represented by Fedd & Company, Inc.

13 14 15 16 17 18 19   7 6 5 4 3 2 1

To my heavenly Father,
for being the ultimate Redeemer

Foreword

by Justin Bieber

My mom is the strongest woman I've ever met. I've always known it, but this book has helped to remind me just how strong she is. I've always admired her. She is an example of a person who doesn't compromise and doesn't quit. Just by who she is, my mom inspires me to be a good man. And she is always pushing me to be better.

I know she has given up a lot and made a ton of sacrifices to be my mother and raise me. And I'm excited to see new things, like this book, unfold in her own life. I might be biased as her son and her biggest fan, but I'm a strong believer that my mom's story is one that needs to be heard. As you read this book, you'll find that her life wasn't easy, as much of her early years were a struggle. It was hard to read about my mom's pain, but I recognize how important it is for her story to be told.

Anyone who has gone through similar experiences needs a little bit of hope—to know there is light at the end of the tunnel. That's what I know my mom can give through this story. As she shares about finding strength and peace, I hope you find the same. I wish you the best in your own journey. Know that God is with you.

I love you, Mom.

A Note from the Author

Thank you for reading my story. Before you dive in, I'd like to share with you my heart and my vision for this book. It's about more than simply me telling about my life, because frankly, there are many parts of my story that I'd rather forget and that I'm certainly not proud of. But there are also instances of amazing grace for which I'm supremely thankful. I decided to tell my story not only for my own healing from a difficult past but also to help bring healing and liberation to those of you who may have suffered in similar ways. A major key in my healing was finding my voice the voice I never had as a little girl. By giving that little girl a voice, I hope to help others find theirs and find the courage to use it. My heart's desire is that my words bring others the hope that I have discovered in my own life.

I write especially for those of you who know the pain of sexual abuse as well as all those who have experienced abandonment, rejection, and fear. I write for those of you who believe you are damaged goods and who identify yourselves by the wounds of your past. I write to encourage you that there is hope, there is light, and there is a life worth living beyond the pains of the past. I write because I believe with my whole heart that you—just like me—can find your way to ultimate healing and freedom.

I ask that you read this book without throwing stones. We're all human and we've all made mistakes. Most of us, however, don't have them aired out for the world to read. Understand that people change, as I have, and everyone deserves grace and a second chance.

I'd like to acknowledge my family and Jeremy for their understanding in how they, and especially some of their vulnerable moments, appear as part of this book. They are part of a bigger picture. Their experiences too can help others for a greater purpose. I honor them for their courage and commend them for their bravery as I recount some hurtful memories.

You'll see that Jeremy and I had a particularly difficult relationship. We were both young and immature when we were together. And I especially want you to know that just as I have changed, Jeremy has too, and he is a different man than he once was. I'm proud of how far he has come as a man and as a father. Today, I consider him a friend.

I'm grateful to all the family members and friends who are part of my story. I love them with all my heart and am thankful beyond words.

one

There are some memories, the painful ones you'd rather forget, that lie still for years. Hauntingly quiet. Crouching behind smiles, laughter, and good times. But eventually even dark secrets must leave their hiding place and come out. And my story has included its share of dark secrets. As I've gotten older, I've needed courage to face those parts of my early years, because sometimes you have to go through your past to get to your future.

My father was an alcoholic who followed in the footsteps of his alcoholic father. I don't know much about my dad because he left when I was two years old. I do know he was violent. My dad even pushed my mom around when she was pregnant with me. I've learned from talking to other family members that my dad was like a chameleon. While others saw him as a loving, charming, and gentle husband and father, we saw his hidden dark side.

My mom, Diane, was the oldest of ten children. She met my dad and got pregnant when she was sixteen. They started a new life together in the city of Timmins, Ontario, Canada, before eventually moving to Stratford, a ten-hour drive away.

My brother, Chris, was born in 1967, followed just eighteen months later by Sally, the sister I never met. When Sally was five years old, her life was tragically cut short when she was hit by a car in the street in front of our house. My mom was four months pregnant with me at the time.

My mom and I haven't always been close, but my heart breaks today when I think about the agonizing grief she went through, the pain that never goes away when you lose a child. And she endured that loss while she was pregnant—how do you mourn one child while preparing to give life to another?

I've often wondered if Sally's death had anything to do with the disconnect I always felt between me and my mother. For years the emotional detachment between the two of us had me convinced I was adopted, because I always felt like I didn't belong.

Every now and then something would drive that powerful feeling to the surface and I'd go on a rampage. I remember one time as a teen when I frantically searched the house for a piece of evidence—anything that would confirm I was adopted. I had convinced myself my birth mother was somewhere out there. And that maybe she was even looking for me.

A strong sense of belonging is one of the greatest needs we have. When we don't have that, our self-esteem and self-worth can begin to crack, especially as teenagers.

I threw open every cupboard in the kitchen, rattling the glasses and china like an aftershock. I opened and slammed shut desk and dresser drawers throughout the house. There had to be something somewhere. Just one measly document. I rummaged through closets, tossing aside old shoes, musty sweaters, and dusty boxes of God-knows-what. I turned the house upside down that day.

Finally, in desperation, I cried to my mom, "I know I'm adopted! Stop lying to me. Just tell me where the papers are. I know it's true."

My mom must have thought I was nuts. "Stop it," she begged. "What are you talking about?" She grabbed a pair of photos and

14

shoved them in my face, comparing our baby pictures side by side. "You look just like me! Why would you even think you're adopted?"

But I couldn't stop thinking about it. And I couldn't calm down. Something in me was still convinced I didn't belong. This was not my home. She was not my mother.

Where did these feelings come from? And why were they so strong?

My feelings of being disconnected didn't just show up out of nowhere. I was two when my dad left us. And his abandonment ripped a hole in my heart—one that began filling with thoughts and feelings that would scar my identity and self-worth.

Today, I can still close my eyes and feel the pain in my heart when he walked out. I was so young, but I still remember it clearly, as if it happened yesterday. In fact, it's my earliest childhood memory.

I remember my brother and me standing by the front door, blinking our big eyes and looking up to our father as he pulled on his jacket. *He looks so serious. Where's he going? Why is he taking a big suitcase? Mommy?* As my dad knelt down before the two of us, he handed me a parting gift, a Thumbelina doll. When I touched her plastic skin and looked into her big eyes that stared back at mine, I decided she was my best friend. As long as I had her, she never left my side.

> Sometimes the greatest wounds aren't the ones others can see on the outside, but the ones we hide on the inside.

"I love you so much," Daddy began. "But I have to move far away." He hugged each of us and slowly stood up, looking like a looming giant next to the toddler me. "I'll always love you."

As he turned his back to me, I could see his big hand pause on the knob of the front door. It felt like an eternity passed before he finally twisted the knob, opened the door, and walked out of our apartment. As the door slowly closed behind him, my heart reached out. I was too confused to actually cry out, but on the inside I was screaming for my dad. *Don't leave! Come back. Please, I need you.* But it was too late. My daddy was gone. I wouldn't see him again until I was nine years old.

> Parents provide our foundation for establishing basic trust as a developing child. That trust lies at the core of self-confidence. When that trust is betrayed, our greatest loss is often the ability to hold our hearts open to love—whether that be love for God, ourselves, or others.

Over the years, I've grieved not having had my dad around to call me Princess, to tell me how beautiful I was, and to threaten the boys I dated. I've mourned the loss of not having a dad I could curl up and feel secure with. A dad who would cherish me. A dad who would remind me that I was worth more than perhaps I believed I was. All little girls (and boys) need that kind of assurance from their dad.

In that moment when I was two years old, though, all I wanted so desperately was to climb into my mother's arms and be soothed by the tenderness only a mother could give. But I couldn't. The day my dad left was the day I had to start growing up. I had to wipe my own tears and pull myself up by the bootstraps. There was no time for sadness. No room for confusion or emotions.

It was also the day I began to learn that my mother, who did an excellent job working hard to provide for and care for our physical needs, wasn't going to give me the kind of warm and fuzzy feelings I longed for. She couldn't. The weight of her own burdens prevented her from giving me the kind of emotional support I needed. My mother was and still is a very strong woman. I, however, didn't have that kind of steel survival strength. Not yet.

Mom remarried when I was six, and I thought I had found my golden ticket. Bruce Dale was quiet, good-natured, and every bit in love with my mother. They were head over heels for each other, stealing kisses every chance they got. When Mom and Bruce were first together, he and I would watch boxing on TV. I'd climb on his lap, unable to take my eyes off of the sweaty boxers exchanging crushing blows, and proudly tell him, "I'm gonna be a boxer one day!" I loved the thought of Bruce becoming my daddy.

Bruce already had two children of his own when he met my mom—Candie, who was thirteen, and Chuck, who was eleven. Candie was a sweetheart and I looked up to her. She was a good big sister and always made time for me and made me feel special. My stepbrother had a gentle nature like his father, and he was fun to be around. I loved them both.

The more I got to know Bruce, the more I liked him. Especially because I knew how well he treated my mother. On August 15, 1981, the day of their wedding, I was so excited I could hardly stand it. My mom looked so pretty with

> Dads are especially important to their daughters as they help to establish their identity. They do this in many ways—through words, protection, emotional support, and spiritual guidance—but especially through their active presence. When dads are not around (as mine wasn't), daughters tend to seek after these things from other male figures or in other unhealthy ways.

her short hair brushed in a soft wave to the side. She wore a turquoise chiffon dress that complemented her eyes and held a small bouquet of beautiful white and pink roses. Bruce stood tall and proud next to her. He looked sharp in his dark brown suit. The boys wore light corduroy jackets with big-collared shirts sticking out like sore thumbs. They looked uncomfortable in their fancy clothes, like they wanted to tear them off and throw on some jeans. Candie and I wore pretty white dresses and matching knee-high socks. I got my hair done and even used hairspray for the first time.

But for me, the wedding was about more than looking pretty. This was my moment. I would have a new dad. A dad who loved me and wanted to stay. I thought this was the best thing that could ever happen to me.

Later, after the wedding, I called out for Bruce, who was in the other room. "Daddy!"

I'd had such a deep longing to say that word. But as soon as I said it, my brother Chris exploded.

Chris pulled me close to him so Bruce couldn't hear what he was about to say. "That is not your dad," he hissed in my face. "That is your mother's husband. He is a stranger in this house. Do not call him Daddy. You already have a dad!"

I didn't understand why Chris was so upset, but I listened to him. And after that, I never did call Bruce "Daddy" again. I've always liked Bruce, but I also looked up to Chris. After all, he was my big brother, so I respected his wishes. But in the process, I missed out on what could have been such a special relationship with my stepdad.

Sadly, I can understand now where Chris was coming from then. He was seven years older than me, so he'd had more time with our dad than I had. Naturally, he felt more of an attachment to our father than I did. And having been the only male in our house for a few years, he may have felt threatened by the new male figure in our home. I don't believe for a second Chris knew how deeply wounding his words were. I'm sure that had he known, he wouldn't have said them.

On that day, though, I immediately created a distance between my stepdad and me. For the rest of my childhood, I never gave Bruce the chance to take on the role of a father. Though I loved him dearly and he never did anything wrong or hurtful, in my eyes he would always be my mother's husband. Not my dad.

two

To look at our family, we were normal—whatever "normal" means (it means something different to everyone). My childhood appeared to be rather uneventful. We lived in a small two-story house that was nestled in a quiet suburban neighborhood in Stratford, Ontario, Canada. My mom and stepdad both worked hard at their blue-collar jobs to provide for our family. Our block was home to kids of all ages, and we played together all the time.

Just about every day someone knocked at my front door to ask if I could come out and play or if they could come in and play with me at my house. And you never had to ask me twice.

I loved playing with my friends. We rode bikes. We hung out at the jungle gym of the elementary school just down the block. I went over to my friends' houses and we ate homemade chocolate chip cookies while making Lite-Brite art, playing with fruity-scented Strawberry Shortcake dolls, or trying to figure out the Rubik's Cube.

My friends and I organized block parades with all the kids in the neighborhood. We even put on plays when we were older. We'd write our own scripts, sell tickets door-to-door, and perform on a makeshift stage.

I had birthday parties with loads of colorful balloons and presents, and I'd always invite all the kids from the neighborhood. I played with Cabbage Patch Kids and stuffed animals. I had silly

> **What is sexual abuse?**
> Sexual abuse is defined as any type of non-consensual (or unwanted) sexual contact, at any age, by one or more persons on another by force, threats, or coercion.

elementary school crushes on boys. When it snowed in the winter (and it snowed a lot!), my siblings and I made snowmen and forts. We took family vacations on occasion; we even went to Florida one year. We hosted our extended family for Thanksgiving and stuffed ourselves with delicious food. We decorated the tree for Christmas and battled the crowds at the malls for presents.

On the outside, it looked like nothing out of the ordinary was going on in my life. But underneath it all, bad stuff was happening. While things looked normal to others, I was enduring many years of sexual abuse.

It started when I was three years old. I can only recall blurry details of the first time, as if the incident happened in a fog. Yet the memory is still there.

I remember lying on a table. Older kids were present, familiar faces. I thought we were playing an innocent game and wasn't

> Anyone can be a victim of sexual abuse. It doesn't matter
>
> - if you're a boy or a girl,
> - how old you are,
> - what your race is,
> - if you come from a rich or poor family, or
> - what part of the world you live in.
>
> It's hard to say for certain how many kids have been sexually abused because so many incidences go unreported. Up to 80,000 cases are reported every year in the United States. As many as 1 in 4 girls and 1 in 6 boys are sexually abused before they turn 18.[1]

prepared for what happened. I was touched in places I shouldn't have been. It felt wrong. And gross.

Strangely, even though I don't have any specific memories of incidents prior to that time, I remember feeling like it had happened before. I don't know for sure about that. What I do know is that it would not be the last time.

I was five when it happened the second time. I knew my molester. He was a familiar face in my circle of family, community, and friends. Someone I should have been able to trust. Trust is broken when someone you know, someone you are supposed to feel safe around and with, does things and makes you do things that hurt and that are wrong.

> Most children who are abused are victimized by someone they know and trust. About 60 percent of perpetrators are known to the child but are not family members (friends, babysitters, etc.). Just 10 percent are strangers.[2]

I was carefully choosing the prettiest crayons to use on the next page of my coloring book when he walked into the room where I played. He wasn't wearing any clothes. The crayon that was just about to shade a colorless sun a warm yellow slipped through my hands and fell to the floor with an echoing thud. I was confused and scared. I was shocked.

I remember being told to do things that were foreign to me. I didn't want to; I just followed his lead. Like a good little girl.

For the next five years, his inappropriate touching continued. And for the next five years, I kept quiet. I was embarrassed. Disgusted. Trying to believe it was a dream or another reality.

Unfortunately, he wasn't the only one. During the same time period a second molester entered my life. Another person I knew and trusted.

In those moments, blinded by shame, I longed for someone to save me or care enough to even notice something bad was happening close by. But no one did. How could they? No one knew what was going on. It was my secret.

The abandonment that overwhelmed my heart as a little girl who watched her daddy walk away was quickly turning into something bigger than me. As I look back, I can see a child who felt sad. Unwanted. Unloved. Unlovable. Those feelings grew like a fungus and made me hungry for attention.

Many child sexual abuse survivors blame themselves. If you are one of these people, know that it's not your fault! You didn't deserve the abuse. You didn't ask for it. And you're not a bad, dirty, or worthless person because it happened to you. You are not damaged goods. You are loving, intelligent, wonderful, and a beautiful person inside and out!

I knew it was wrong for others to touch me in intimate places, but in a warped way I didn't mind so much. Don't misunderstand me—I didn't *like* what was happening. But I wanted so desperately to feel loved and wanted. No matter what it looked like, no matter where it came from.

I was sexually violated so many times by so many different kinds of abusers—young and old, male and female, familiar faces and strangers—that as the years went by it began to feel normal.

When I think about some of the events today, it's like an explosion goes off and I see one moment frozen in time. One scene. One

There's no way around it: children are shaped, for better or worse, by their parents. There are certain things every one of us needs and deserves from our parents when we are children: to be given love, affection, protection, a sense of belonging, freedom, limits, and guidance.

foggy face. I know what's happening, but I don't see every single detail. I've learned that's normal. Like most victims of sexual abuse, I had to forget some parts of the events in order to survive. It's a defense mechanism. My mind wouldn't allow me to remember the play-by-play because I couldn't handle it. Most people can't.

But some things are impossible to forget.

In the moments of abuse, I learned how to clench my eyes tight and hold my breath until it was over.

> A sexually abused child almost always accepts the guilt for the abuse. Some of the deepest shame, guilt, and self-hatred occur because aspects of the abuse felt good. Often the child senses that something is "wrong" or "weird," but their body is designed to respond to sensual and sexual touch with pleasure. This confusing but pleasurable feeling in no way implies that the victim wanted to be abused or enjoyed the abuse.

I tried not to think about how uncomfortable and scared I was or how I wanted to crawl inside of myself and disappear. I just held on for dear life to emptiness, a blank mind, and a heart void of feelings.

Though my experiences taught me to shut down, I couldn't escape the burning desire to be unconditionally loved the way I wanted—for the love I needed from my mom and dad.

From the day my dad left I missed him. And I wanted him back. As a little girl, I waited for the day the phone would ring and it would be him. I had the script memorized. He'd talk about how he'd been flooded with remorse and regret for leaving us, and he'd tell me how much he loved me and that he was coming back and staying for good. He'd repeat "I'm sorry" until the words mended my broken heart and rid me of the sadness I had carried all those years.

As the years went by, my dream of being reunited with him started to fade. By the time I was nine, I had just a pinch of hope left. But I still loosely held on to the fantasy of being rescued by him, especially because I had not connected on an emotional level with any other adult, including my mom or stepdad.

I came home from school one day that year and bounced through the front door. On my way to the kitchen to grab a snack, I noticed my mom sitting on the couch with a strange man. They spoke quietly. The tension was obvious. My mom's shoulders were uncomfortably stiff and the man looked nervous.

> If one of your parents walked out on you, it's okay to feel anger, grief, sadness, or confusion. And it's important to remember you are not the reason they left. Adults are responsible for the actions they take. You are never responsible for a parent abandoning you.

When she saw me, my mom stood up and smoothed her pants. "Pattie," she began in a monotone voice. "This is Mike . . . your father." The tall, skinny man beside my mother stood up. I felt so tiny next to him. It was like looking up at a skyscraper. He looked nervous and kept fiddling with his hands. This was him? The man I'd waited for my whole life?

I blinked. A lot. I was caught off guard. No matter how many times I had pictured this moment in my head, I wasn't prepared. I wasn't sure how to react. I definitely felt a jolt of excitement; the butterflies in my stomach were flying into each other. But I couldn't move. My feet were glued to the floor.

My dad looked into my eyes and smiled. "Hello, Pattie," he said. He was kind and seemed genuine, but the moment wasn't anything like the reunion I'd played out in my head for the past seven years. We didn't have a sappy TV moment with each other, but things weren't totally awkward either. Actually, we were comfortable enough to go out to eat that evening with my brother, Chris. The three of us went to the mall afterward, and my dad bought me a soft E.T. doll. I was thrilled. It replaced Thumbelina, who had been hijacked and destroyed by my brother not long after my dad gave her to me.

Over the years, I had wondered what happened to my dad— whether he got married and had more kids, what kind of new life he started for himself. But for a long time, I was too deeply buried in feelings of abandonment and rejection to really think about those things. I was consumed with questions: What's wrong with me? Why am I not good enough? Why didn't I matter?

I think at one point I asked my mom about what happened to my dad, and she told me she thought he did get married but didn't have any more children of his own. Honestly, I think the rejection I felt would have been a lot worse if he did have kids.

When my dad and I reunited that day after so many years, him being back was so new and shocking that I didn't really focus on having been rejected so many years back. I was starting to get excited about having my daddy back.

That night after our dinner and trip to the mall, my dad returned home to Timmins, a ten-hour drive away. But he promised to keep in touch. After the shock wore off, I was beside myself. My dad was back. I was on cloud nine that I was going to have a relationship with him. I mattered again. This was my moment, and nothing could take him away from me. Nothing.

My dad kept his promise to stay in touch. I remember getting phone calls from him every now and then. He even mailed me the best gift ever. I had been begging my mom for cable TV in my room, but we didn't have a cable outfit upstairs. My father mailed me the longest cable cord I have ever seen in my entire life so I could connect my TV to the downstairs line. (Can you imagine needing a cable that long for your TV? Technology is a lot different today than when I was a kid.) My mother wasn't happy because the cable had to run from the first floor living room up the stairs, through the hall, and into my room. I, on the other hand, was ecstatic. Cable in my room! Wow!

A few months after my dad's visit, my brother had made plans to spend the summer with my dad, his wife, and his extended family. Chris was supposed to leave early in the morning, about the time my mom got a phone call. I didn't hear the phone ring, but I did hear the door to my bedroom creak open and my mom walk over to my bed. I was groggy, still in a sleep fog. It was only six thirty in the morning.

"Pattie, I'm sorry," she told me. "Your father died last night. He had a heart attack."

It was strange. I felt nothing. It was like almost at the sound of those words, my heart instantly turned off. That last bit of hope I had about my dad coming back vanished.

As I'd done time and time again in the past, I detached myself emotionally to protect myself from feeling even the slightest bit of emotion. I did, however, feel sorry for my mom and ask her if she was okay. She said she was fine, which made me feel that I too

Many children who have been hurt disconnect from their feelings because it's easier. It's also a built-in coping mechanism we have to survive traumatic situations.

I know how scary it is to admit and face things like fear, worry, and pain. But trust me, if you bury your feelings instead of dealing with them and talking to someone about them, they will only grow deeper.

When you bury pain, it comes out in all kinds of ways, like sickness or rebellion. When you finally admit and face your feelings, you will begin to find healing.

should feel fine. It seemed emotions were messy, an inconvenience. Better not to have any, I guess. No muss. No fuss.

Six years later, I went to visit my dad's grave in Timmins. Most of our relatives on both sides lived there, so our family made the drive at least once a year to visit. On a clear sunny day during one of those visits, I stood in front of his tombstone and yelled at the top of my lungs.

For about an hour, I screamed at the slab of stone in hopes of surfacing the emotions I knew were inside of me. I was angry. I had spent my childhood stuffing down emotion, shoving aside my hurts and pains, pushing raw feelings down so deep that I had trouble digging them out. I stared at the tombstone bearing my father's name and yelled at him for leaving me too early, for abandoning me twice. But even as the words flew out of my mouth so effort-lessly, I wasn't really emotional. I was still so far removed from the deepest part of my heart.

I was so hurt by the abuse, rejection, and disappointment I'd experienced that the only way I could live a normal (whatever that means) life was to disconnect. Abuse? Disconnect. Emotionally absent mom? Disconnect. Dad dies? Disconnect. It wasn't long before those defenses worked against me. Being a pro at discon-necting did, however, give me one advantage.

My ability to disconnect from reality helped fuel my love for the arts, especially acting. I always thought I was going to be an actress. When I was around nine, I made appearances on *Romper Room* and *Big Top Talent*, a Canadian television children's talent show where I recited a monologue from *Anne of Green Gables* and told the story of Jack and the Beanstalk. I was a ham who loved not just the camera but pretending I was someone else.

I'm sure I was drawn to acting because it allowed me to step away from what was happening to me. It also gave me a sense of control. I could use my voice to make people laugh or cry. I could be as loud and dramatic as I wanted. I could even sing.

I loved to sing. All through middle school and high school, I took every drama and choir class that was offered. I was in the school choir every year and had major roles in almost every school play. I was quite literally a drama queen. I also spent seven years taking dance lessons. I couldn't get enough of the arts.

When I was ten, I performed in the Stratford Shakespeare Festival, a celebration of the theatrical arts that runs from April to November every year. More than half a million tourists from all over the world visit our little town during that time to see wonderful performances of plays by Shakespeare and other greats. I was cast for two roles in *The Government Inspector* and played a peasant girl and a rich girl.

I loved the hustle backstage before the performance—sitting in the hair and makeup chair, wearing frilly costumes, being doted on by the older actresses. But being onstage thrilled me even more. It gave me a sense of freedom. My heart wasn't burdened by feelings of abandonment, fear, or rejection or by those wretched dirty feelings I still didn't understand. I was free to act, to be dramatic and perform from a place in my spirit that held innocence.

Throughout elementary and middle school, I filled up my bedroom with awards and trophies from singing and acting competitions. I even got accepted into an acting agency in Toronto, but it required me going to auditions on the weekend. My mom and Bruce couldn't make the hour-and-a-half drive, so I had to pass up the opportunity. I was devastated. It was the one chance I'd had to develop something I was actually really good at. My dreams were crushed.

As much as I loved acting and drawing from different identities and personas, I still couldn't escape how others were violating my body.

I felt trapped in the silence, not knowing it was okay to use my voice and say no.

I was ten when a thirty-second public service announcement (PSA) helped me find my power. I was mindlessly watching TV when a pint-sized African American boy whom I knew as Webster from the TV show of the same name talked to me as he moved through a set of giant, colorful letters of the alphabet.

My ears started ringing when I heard, "Sometimes grown-ups touch kids in ways they don't like."

It was the first time I had ever heard someone say exactly what I had been feeling for the last five-plus years. This kid knew how I felt. My heart started beating wildly in my chest. I thought it was going to break through my skin and take off like a rocket. Then I heard the voice of another little kid in the background who mentioned something about his uncle touching him in an icky way. *Yes!* I wanted to shout through the screen. *Yes, that's right! It feels icky. It feels gross.*

The kid continued to talk about feeling funny when someone touches you and tells you not to tell anyone else. And then Emmanuel Lewis said the magic words that gave me a way to put a stop to the abuse. That gave me my voice.

> Sexual abuse robs a person of innocence, power, and usually his or her voice. The key to getting back your power is to recognize you have a voice and begin to use it. When you say no and tell a trusted adult what is happening, the abuse starts to lose its power.

"Say no. Then go. And tell someone you trust."

My mind raced. So many different thoughts cluttered my brain in that moment. *All I have to do is say no? Is it really that easy? Will it work?*

I was nervous but desperate enough to try it out. I knew the touching had to stop.

I sat numbly in front of the TV as the show I had been watching continued. I started to feel afraid, thinking of all the reasons I shouldn't say no and should continue to keep quiet. *What if I say no and he gets mad? What if me saying no makes him hurt me? What if I say no and he rejects me and never talks to me again?*

But my biggest fear was, *What if it just doesn't work?*

In the end, I knew I had to do it. I knew I had to say no. The PSA gave me just enough courage to try.

I know that in many cases just saying no won't stop the abuse. That's why it's important to tell someone you trust who will listen and help.

One day it happened. I came face-to-face with my original molester. When he approached me, I mustered up all the courage I could find and meekly said, "No. I don't want this to happen anymore." My voice was barely above a whisper, as loud as I was able to speak. But my message was clear: no.

Then I said it a second time, a tiny notch louder.

"No."

What happened next amazes me to this day. He nodded, said, "Okay," and walked out of the room. He never touched me again.

I found myself in the same situation again a few weeks later, with the other longtime offender. When that young man started his own ritual with me, I whispered my conviction in that same quiet voice. "No," I told him, just as I had the other guy. "I don't want to do this anymore." And with that, he never again laid a hand on me.

Finally, I had found my voice. And I found bits and pieces of just enough strength to use it.

What I didn't do, however, was tell anyone about what had happened. I didn't understand why I had to tell someone I trusted. None of my abusers had ever explicitly told me not to tell anyone.

If you have been sexually abused, tell someone. And keep telling until someone listens and helps you. Don't be embarrassed or allow shame to keep you silent. Use your voice and get help.

Tell your parents or an adult you trust like a teacher, guidance counselor, or youth pastor. Or call one of the hotlines listed in the back of this book.

If you know someone who is being abused, tell a trusted adult or notify local authorities. Don't ignore sexual abuse just because it's not happening to you.

I just didn't. Why would I want to, anyway? There was no need for someone else to know about my unbearable shame.

During the few seconds it took to say no, I was a part of the present. I wasn't distant. I didn't unplug. I didn't close my eyes and pretend time had stopped and bad things weren't happening. I acknowledged that things weren't right. That what was happening to me had to stop.

While the word *no* was my permission slip to speak up and defend myself, I quickly learned the word wasn't magic. Damage had already been done.

three

I spent most of my early teen years in my bedroom, zoned out
from the rest of the world and from my dark memories. I buried
my head in my journals, where I would furiously write about how
life sucked and how miserable I was. I struggled with depression,
a battle I'd fight well into my adulthood. I didn't know how to
deal with my pain, so I wrote poem after poem, every one of them
telling the story of a girl with a broken heart. My words painted
the picture of an identity crisis, my obvious depression, and hints
of confusion about my sexual trauma.

> I try so hard
> To be what others want me to be.
> I am forever being someone else,
> And for this, I know not who I am . . .
> It hurts to pretend.
> I feel as if I don't fit in anywhere . . .
> I am responsible for things I do and decisions
>   I make,
> But wrong choices are made and disaster occurs.
> When things are built up inside,
> Whether it be frustration, anger, or confusion,
> The thought of suicide is possible to occur . . .

Four percent of adolescents will develop significant symptoms of serious depression each year in the United States.

For every 33 children in school, one child will have clinical depression.

Being depressed is different than being occasionally sad or having the blues. Here are some signs of depression:

- Continual feelings of guilt, shame, worthlessness, hopelessness, anger, irritability
- No or low energy levels and motivation
- Difficulty concentrating
- Social withdrawal
- Negative thinking

If you or someone you know is experiencing these symptoms, tell your parents, a teacher, or a counselor and seek professional help.[3]

No one knew the kinds of destructive things that festered in my heart. Outside of seeing me act out in rebellion, a little at first, my family probably didn't even have a clue something was wrong. You want the ones who are supposed to love you the most to take the time to look beyond your messy parts or rough edges, but I didn't feel like my mom or stepdad were interested in doing that. To be fair, I guess it's hard enough for a parent to deal with a teenager, let alone understand a broken one. I just felt they didn't even try.

Aside from sitting at the table during meals, our family rarely spent time together. By this time all my siblings were out of the house, so at times I felt pretty lonely at home. I may not have acted like it, but I would have liked to do stuff as a family, even if it was just Bruce, my mom, and me. Stuff like taking bike rides. Or having a family game night. Or going to a sporting event. But we didn't do much together other than watch TV.

Communication wasn't a big deal in our family. Outside of small talk about boring topics like the weather or school, we really didn't talk a whole lot. We definitely didn't share our feelings openly with each other.

I know my mother recognized the tension between us. She even admitted at times she didn't know how to relate to or talk with me. But recognizing the tension didn't fix it.

Like any kid who has been through a traumatic experience, I was left screaming on the inside with overwhelming angst. I wanted so badly to let go and talk about everything that had been locked inside my heart, all the ugliness and all the shame. I was dying to tell my mother about the injustices I had faced, about feeling alone, about being scared. But I didn't know how to. And unfortunately, most of what I *did* say came out as yelling and was disrespectful.

Sometimes I approached my mom with tears in my eyes after I got into a fight with one of my friends or was bullied, but her response was always the same. Time and time again she told me, "I

Most teenagers have conflict with their parents. But while it's normal, it's no excuse not to try to have a healthy relationship with your mom or dad. Here are some ways you can help make that happen:

- Communicate in a healthy way.
- Be honest. Keep your word and don't lie.
- Don't get mad if your parents hold you accountable for poor choices you make.
- Be responsible. Let them know they can trust you.
- Treat them with respect. Don't call them names or slam doors in their face.
- Stay calm. Don't get swept up in emotions.

don't know how to do this, Pattie. My mom never talked to me, so I don't know how to talk to you. Just talk to a guidance counselor or one of your friends' moms. I love you, but I just can't talk to you."

> It's just as important for parents to talk to their children as it is for children to talk to their parents.

It wasn't that my mom didn't care. She just doesn't naturally show love through words or affection; she shows love by doing things for others. While I was growing up, my mom worked full-time in a factory. But she always came home and made time to cook for us, do laundry, get what we needed for school, make sure the house was in order, and provide what she could that we needed. (My mom still loves to do these things for me when I visit with her in Canada.)

Today I can better understand and appreciate my mom's particular ways of loving me, but the fact is, when I was a teenager, it hurt. I couldn't talk to her about things that were important to me, like how I felt when my dad left. That was a big one. His leaving was traumatic.

Along the way I came to some pretty unhealthy conclusions: I wasn't important. My feelings weren't valid. My thoughts didn't matter. So I learned how to cope with what I couldn't handle on my own by stuffing it inside. I locked the most upsetting and traumatizing events in a place so deep, I hoped I'd never be able to dig them out.

When I was in the eighth grade, I started hanging out with a group of girls who were always getting in trouble for something. Stealing was our cheap thrill. We especially got a kick out of stealing ketchup chips (popular in Canada) and Zesty Cheese Doritos out of the school cafeteria. I know, big deal! (Wanna hear a really embarrassing secret between you and me? My friends and I called ourselves the Chipettes. How cheesy is that?)

The six of us thought we were big shots, rebels without a clue. We were joined at the hip and did everything together. We had slumber parties. We swapped clothes. We pined after cute boys. We complained about our parents. We hated school. And, of course, we got off on our small-town criminal activity, like stealing chips and, when we were feeling super cocky, cheap red lipsticks from the local drugstore. Five of us also loved to sing and were involved with the school tour choir.

One day the choir was scheduled to perform a concert at a huge mall in London, Ontario. People all over the mall—looking for great sales, trying to find the perfect pair of jeans, hanging out at the food court you could smell from the level below—would hear our catchy pop tunes. The five of us were excited about performing, but mostly we were psyched about spending a school day at a mall.

I sensed something weird, though, on the bus ride there. I sat on a two-seater by myself while my best friends sat across from me. The girls chatted away in their private world, leaning into each other at such an angle that I couldn't help but feel they were ignoring me. They nodded my way every so often as I tried to force my way into their conversation. They were polite but not really friendly like BFFs are. It felt awkward. And I felt left out.

Did I do something wrong? Did I say something wrong?

As the bus bounced along the highway, the massive billboards and gray office buildings flashing by, my hurt feelings grew deeper. I ignored the rest of the choir as they loudly belted out their singing parts, preparing for the big debut. When the bus finally rolled into the mall parking lot, my friends barged their way to the front of the bus, leaving me to walk real fast to keep up.

We had an hour to walk around before we had to meet to line up for the concert. The teachers barked out orders, reminding us not to be even a minute late, then finally gave us permission to go. We were like stallions being released into the wild, or in this case, into a bunch of stores where we could drool over the coolest shoes or pair of shades.

While I stood in the middle of my best friends, I couldn't ignore the tension, like they were almost forcing themselves to be in my presence. I noticed they were looking at each other with knowing glances. Finally they nudged one of the girls forward to face me. She looked sheepish, uncomfortable, and couldn't look into my eyes. It was obvious she didn't want to say what she was about to but knew there was no way around it.

> Being rejected by your peers, especially your friends, hurts. Teenagers have an inherent need to feel accepted and like they belong. And when that doesn't happen, it can crush you. Talk to someone about what you are going through. Don't stuff your feelings inside like I did. It will only make you feel worse. Surround yourself with friends who truly care about you, not what you look like, what you wear, or how much money you have.

"We don't want to hang out with you today, Pattie." She paused and raised her eyes to the ceiling before letting out a deep sigh. "And, well, we don't want you to hang out with us anymore or be our friend."

The words punched me in the gut. The blow was sharp and traveled further and deeper than just being told someone didn't want to be my friend. It struck a familiar chord at a level I didn't even know existed. My eyes welled with tears.

Another one of my so-called friends quickly piped up. She sounded more confident and not at all apologetic. "Yeah, and don't go crying like a baby."

I panicked. My mind went into overdrive. "What did I do wrong?" I asked. "Was it something I said? Or did? Give me a chance to fix it. I'm so sorry . . ." My voice trailed off in a stuttering mess of apologies. I felt like they had just poured a pound of salt over the already open wound of rejection.

> It makes me sad, but the world is full of mean girls (and boys). Did you know a girl is bullied every 7 minutes, whether it's in the schoolyard, playground, stairwell, classroom, or bathroom?[4] Cyberbullying is a big problem also:
>
> - 42 percent of kids have been bullied while online, and 1 in 4 have had it happen more than once.
> - 35 percent of kids have been threatened online, and nearly 1 in 5 have had it happen more than once.
> - 21 percent of kids have received mean or threatening email or other messages.[5]
>
> It's no wonder kids struggle with depression, low self-esteem, and substance abuse.

Just as the tears were about to pour, I clenched my jaw and used every ounce of strength I could find to keep myself from crying. I was proud of myself. My eyes welled so much I could barely see, but not one tear dropped. Not one.

I knew what I had to do: Pull myself up. Be strong. Keep it together. Pretend as if that conversation never happened. I was good at that kind of pretending by now. It was how I coped.

I ended up walking around by myself, aimlessly wandering through the mall. I was devastated. Utterly and absolutely devastated. But I wouldn't let my true feelings show.

Though it may seem like a silly event today, the sting of that rejection stuck with me through the years. It confirmed, in my mind, that I wasn't important. That I didn't matter. That nobody wanted me, not even my best friends.

The next year, my rebellious streak grew stronger. There's no way around it. I was a troublemaker. The more bad things I did, the less I cared. The first time I stole something, a chocolate bar, I felt

Nearly all high school students (97 percent) say that classmates drink, use drugs, or smoke. They say that 47 percent of their classmates drink alcohol, 40 percent of their classmates use drugs, and 30 percent smoke.[6]

so guilty. But after stealing a few more chocolate bars and then other more expensive things, I became quite good at ignoring the guilt. I stopped listening to the whispers of my conscience.

I kept pushing boundaries with authority figures, picking fights with teachers and spending most of my after-school hours in detention. But I also moved on to bigger and badder things. I started vandalizing school property; one time I even got suspended for five days because I started a fire in a bathroom. Of course, I didn't mind not having to show up at school that week. I rarely did anyway. Classes were an inconvenience to me. I barely passed, I skipped school so much.

Then came the drugs and alcohol.

I started drinking alcohol and smoking pot when I was fourteen. There were more parties than I knew what to do with, and every one of them featured some type of mind-numbing substance.

To tell the truth, I can't remember the first time I drank or smoked pot. It certainly wasn't that memorable. Since all of my friends were drinking and drugging, it was easy to get sucked in with the crowd, and no one needed to twist my arm to try anything at least once. Besides, Stratford was such a small city. It's easy to get bored when there's not much to do outside of going to malls, hockey games, and parties where parents aren't home. Drugs and alcohol were like an extracurricular activity. It seemed harmless at first—just feeling loopy and doing stupid things—but it didn't stay that way for long.

Around the same time I started experimenting with drugs and alcohol, an old ghost came back into town. It had been about four years since anyone had touched me inappropriately.

I was fourteen years old, it was summer, and I was hanging out with my best friend, one of the infamous Chipettes. We were like sisters, and I often spent time with her family. That summer we spent a week in the great outdoors on a camping adventure with her grandfather and sister. I had seen him around a lot and always felt comfortable with him. He was the kind of grandfather everyone loved—super cuddly and soft, like a big teddy bear you just wanted to wrap your arms around.

I loved hanging out with my friend's grandfather. He was warm and caring, and he loved to give hugs. Because I was so tiny—only four foot six and maybe seventy pounds at the time—there were even times I'd curl up in his lap.

My friend and I spent the first few days of our vacation enjoying nature. We rode bikes, took long hikes, and swam in the campground pool. At night we sat around an inviting fire roasting marshmallows and listening to music.

One afternoon I saw my friend's grandfather sitting on a huge lawn chair, staring into the sky and enjoying the warm breeze. He looked so peaceful. Content. Just breathing in the summer without a care in the world. I wanted to be a part of that beautiful and peaceful picture.

I climbed onto his lap and rested my head in the crook of his leathery neck. He smiled, eyes still closed, and patted my head reassuringly. It wasn't long before I started drifting off to sleep.

And then I felt it—the heat from his warm hand. It was happening again. I was startled as he tried to place his hand inside my shorts. I had to get out of there. Fast.

I let out a fake yawn and stretched, as if I had just woken up from a catnap. Then I got up and stumbled away, pretending I was still drowsy. Pretending nothing ever happened.

I walked back to the camper, the sun blinding me and blasting me with its heat. I felt as if I were trudging through a barren desert, miles away from civilization. The truth was, I was miles away from myself. Once again, I detached from the colorful scene in front of me. I could barely make out the families grilling food, the little kids tossing Frisbees, the worn-out hikers returning from their long walk. I walked in a fog, stunned by what had just happened.

The old familiar feelings came back as if they had never left. But really, they'd been hiding, waiting for the perfect time to reappear. I immediately reconnected with my past abuse and the old memories came back in an explosion. I felt dirty and disgusting.

The event was so upsetting, I tried to convince myself the incident was a fluke. Maybe I had imagined it all.

But I didn't dream it up. It happened. And I finally found enough courage in that moment to tell someone.

Sadly, if you are being abused, there may be times when even though you find the courage to speak up, you are not believed. I know how devastating that is. No matter how strong your instinct is to back off and stay silent, don't! You'll never find peace if you keep quiet or pretend nothing happened. Find someone who will listen to you. Don't give up.

When I got back to the camper, I pulled aside my friend and told her and her sister what had happened. She didn't believe me. Both she and her sister accused me of lying.

I didn't expect that kind of a response. Their reaction devastated me. The PSA I'd seen all those years ago hadn't prepared me for the possibility that I could tell someone but they wouldn't believe me. What then? How do you handle being called a liar when you are the victim?

I wanted to leave the campground immediately after opening up to my friend, but for some reason I stayed. I was used to spending time around my abusers, pretending nothing had ever happened, so it was easy to do.

Later that night, while the four of us played cards, my friend's grandfather made another inappropriate move toward me under the table. It was the final straw. Still not wanting to make a scene, I got up and said I wasn't feeling well and was going to bed. I didn't want—or rather I didn't know how—to handle the situation any other way. I did what was most comfortable: I retreated.

I think that happens a lot with abuse victims. Instead of using our voice to speak out, we keep quiet. We hide. We ignore. We pretend. There are so many different reasons we don't tell others. We feel

> If you were sexually abused as a child, the emotional effects can last a long time and can carry with them self-destructive behaviors. For some, the aftermath of the trauma can last for years. If it has been a while, even years, since you were abused, it's not too late. The time is now. Don't wait another minute longer. Don't waste more precious time. It's time to get your life back. Take the first step and tell someone you trust or call a crisis hotline.

ashamed and embarrassed even though it's not our fault. We don't want to rock the boat. We don't want to make anyone mad. What if they think we asked for it? What if we look stupid? What if they think we're lying?

Though talking feels like it carries too much of a risk, when we keep silent, we dig a deeper grave for ourselves day by day. In carrying the weight of pain, shame, and guilt, we are forced to find other ways to help us deal with it. Usually they are unhealthy ones that lead us further down into a dark hole, making it harder to find our way up.

As a teen, I envied people who could be unguarded, unafraid, free in their spirits and their hearts. I even wrote about that in my journal: "I think [I'm getting] more open with my feelings. I wish someone could understand what I'm going through. In drama class, everyone is so open. Girls told the class how they got abused sexually and a couple raped. It was so sad. Everyone was crying."

Yet in the next sentence, I made a sharp U-turn from writing about being vulnerable and wrote, "I hate how people are popular because they are pretty." I was so removed from the pain in my past, not even my diary knew the depths of my wounds.

Not long after the camping incident, I was drinking and doing drugs every day. I was getting into even more trouble at school and going to parties almost every night. I rarely ate dinner at home, and I never made curfew. Some nights I even stayed out until the early hours of the morning.

Getting drunk and high for fun turned into a means of self-medicating. I couldn't get through a class at school or a holiday function with my family without being stoned or drunk. By the time I was sixteen, I couldn't function at all without numbing myself in some way.

Though my mom and I didn't see each other much because I was either out partying or holed up in my room, when we did, it was like World War III. I spewed mini volcanoes of anger at her, even at her reasonable demands to clean my room or put away my laundry. She might as well have asked me to comb the Sahara Desert. My mom didn't take kindly to my bad attitude and rage and constantly threatened to kick me out of the house.

> *"Man seeks to escape himself in myth, and does so by any means at his disposal. Drugs, alcohol, or lies. Unable to withdraw into himself, he disguises himself. Lies and inaccuracy give him a few moments of comfort."*
>
> —Jean Cocteau,
> *Diary of an Unknown*

One of our fights even got physical. I can't remember what we were arguing about. We exchanged heated words like a ball in a Ping-Pong match. At one point I got in my mom's face. It was too close for comfort. She took a step back and slapped me. The blow made me even angrier, and I threatened to call the cops. I even grabbed the telephone and with a menacing look on my face yelled, "That's it, I'm dialing!"

My mother wasn't one to back down. She called my bluff and grabbed me by the wrist, pulling me toward the front door. "I have a better idea. I'll take you down to the police station myself." And she did.

Down at the station, I had a sit-down with one of the police officers. He talked to me about the importance of respecting my parents, respecting myself, and getting good grades. He was nice, though I can't say his talk made me change my ways or even scared me, as my mother had probably intended.

That was my first experience with the police, but it wouldn't be my last. It wasn't too long before the police started showing up at my house when things like car stereos went missing. They knew the kind of friends I hung out with and the kind of stuff we did. It was obvious—I was on the fast track heading to nowhere.

four

W hen you're broken, it's hard to tell the difference between truth and lies. You believe certain things that hurt you, not build you up. The deeper these untruths stay buried in your heart, the harder it is to get rid of them.

I was bound by so many lies by the time I was a teenager. At best, I had a messed-up idea of love, worth, and self-respect; at worst, I had none. Instead of believing in myself, I hung on to every negative word spoken to me and entertained every taunting thought of my own that surfaced in my mind.

I recently read journal entries from my teen years, and I can't believe the things I called myself. *Lazy. Fat. Ugly.* I even wrote that someone must have been brain damaged to like me. I took to heart the mean things that others said about me—when my so-called friends told me I talked too much or when they spread rumors about me in school. I didn't think so highly of myself either, though. Without much self-worth, I didn't have positive truths to defend against the negative words or even what I said about myself.

When it came to guys, I was always trying to find "the one." But I couldn't seem to make up my mind. I liked Guy X one week, Guy Y the next, and so on. I didn't flip-flop from one guy to the next just because my teenage hormones were out of control, though. I was always searching, trying to find love. Trying to find something real. Trying to find the person who would love me back the way I thought I needed. Getting that from a guy seemed the easiest thing to do.

I fell in love—or like, or whatever it was—easily. And when it didn't last, I was crushed for a long time. When I was fifteen, I found a boy I thought I was going to marry. I'll call him Joey.

I liked this guy a lot. One night after everyone left a party at his house, we sat and cuddled for hours. In the still of the early morning, he started saying all the things a girl wants to hear. "Pattie, you are so beautiful." "You're so soft." "You're so amazing." I swallowed his sweet nothings hook, line, and sinker. I was a hopeless romantic, and his words made me weak in the knees.

> I wish that instead of believing lies about myself, I would have known the truth that . . .
>
> - I am beautiful.
> - I am worthy of being loved.
> - I am smart.
> - I am valuable.
> - I am unique.
> - I am enough.

We started kissing and ended up in his bedroom. I was nervous. I didn't want this to end the way it was obviously going. Despite the amount of abuse I had endured, I was still a virgin. That part of me was precious and innocent.

While I wasn't ready to give up that part of myself, Joey had other ideas. My repeated "nos" fell on deaf ears. He didn't respect my wishes to stop. Immediately, I reverted back into abuse mode. I was still. Silent. Detached from my body. Detached from Joey. Detached from time.

When it was over, I reconnected my body with my mind. I plugged my emotions back in. Though I didn't know it at the time, delusion set in. I repainted the scenario in new colors. In reality, I'd just been robbed of my virginity. But in my new, improved version, I had just been intimate with the man I was going to marry.

No means no. It's not okay for a guy to force himself on you. If someone forces you to have sex, it's rape. If you have been raped:

- Go to a safe place.
- Notify the police.
- Call a friend, family member, or someone you can trust.
- Seek medical attention as soon as possible.
- Talk with a counselor experienced in rape crisis.

I had myself so convinced of this that I walked home on cloud nine. Floating on air. Head over heels in love. I was sure Joey was "the one." I was so excited that I'd finally found the man who was going to make my dreams come true, the man I was going to spend the rest of my life with.

The most traumatic thing about that experience for me wasn't even that I'd been raped; it was what happened the next day when I called Joey to say hello and to see how our "relationship" was going. My dream guy was so mean. Nothing like the night before. Joey immediately cut off my babbling and quietly said, "Please don't call me again."

Click.

The dial tone buzzed in my ear.

I was beyond devastated. I cried my heart out that day and for weeks afterward. I decided I hated Joey and I hated men. The rejection hurt me on such a deep level. It shattered my hope. It scarred my view of love.

Many girls find themselves attracted to the wrong kind of guy, like the "bad boys," because deep down, they really believe that's all they are worth.

49

Not long after the incident with Joey, I met a guy named Jeremy at a party. I walked into a room where a song was blaring, and my eyes immediately landed on a guy doing the "running man." I thought he looked ridiculous doing the dance; I'm sure he thought he looked pretty cool. I didn't see him again until a few weeks later.

We crossed paths off and on for a while, usually at parties. One time we climbed onto the roof of someone's house and talked about nothing and everything for hours. I thought he was a hottie—he had a chiseled body, dreamy eyes, and a handsome face—but I still wasn't totally into him in the beginning. The more I got to know him, however, the deeper I fell. Before I knew it, Jeremy had become my life.

It was almost impossible for me not to fall madly in love with him. And it was equally impossible for anyone not to like him. He was a cool guy, adventurous and spontaneous. He'd pick me up and take me on long walks by the railroad tracks. We'd hitchhike to the city of London, an hour away, to get away from Stratford. I always felt safe with Jeremy, no matter where I was. He was naturally protective, though many times he took that impulse too far.

When two people enter into a relationship and are not whole but in need of healing, they look to the other person to fill the other half of their cup, to make them feel fulfilled and loved. The result is a dysfunctional relationship. First we need to be healed and filled with Jesus. Then we're able to give and love.

On the flip side, Jeremy and I were young and immature and didn't have much working in our favor. We both came from broken homes and didn't know how to love ourselves. As much as we tried, we would never be able to figure out how to love each other. We were doomed from the start.

50

Not every relationship is meant to be. Here are some warning signs of an unhealthy relationship: excessive jealousy, inability to listen, lack of trust, substance abuse, lack of respect, controlling attitude, abusive behavior (physical, psychological, or emotional).

What makes a healthy relationship? Mutual respect, trust, honesty, support, more good times than bad, similar morals and values, healthy communication, outside friends and activities.

Jeremy and I both had our issues. The majority of our on-again, off-again four-year relationship would be unhealthy, suffocated by mind games and distorted by insecurities. We danced to the tune of breaking up and getting back together so many times that a lot of those four years have blurred into each other. I can't even remember anymore when we were actually together and when we were on a "break."

At home, my fights with my mother continued, one after another. It didn't seem like there was a time when we weren't at each other's throats. Finally, when I was sixteen and when Jeremy and I were "off again," I hit a breaking point. I decided to move out.

You'd think it would have been a big moment. I mean, I was still a minor. But I don't remember any drama surrounding my exit. Things had gotten so bad that I think when I left, my mom was more relieved than anything. She and Bruce could finally have a peaceful, calm, and quiet house. Frankly, they deserved that much. Looking back, I'm sure my mother worried about me, though. How could she not?

While my mom and my stepdad regained a sense of normalcy at home, I moved in with some older friends. It was a typical party house with people coming in and out all the time, hanging out and partying. The fridge was always empty except for beer and ketchup. The kitchen was a disaster—plastic garbage bags filled with empty bottles and pizza boxes littering the floor. No amount of Lysol could mask the stale stench in the air. But it was home, and there was nobody to yell at me and get me upset.

School still wasn't a priority. I went every now and then, when I felt like it. When I did show up, I was stoned or drunk or both. When I didn't go, I was either sleeping or partying. The schedule was pretty consistent: Party at night until 6:00 a.m. Sleep all day. Party at night until 6:00 a.m. Sleep all day. I know, very inspiring.

I worked odd jobs to get money for rent and to fuel my drug habit. I worked the midnight shift as a cashier in a gas station for a while. As a night owl, I loved the hours.

All kinds of customers showed up in the wee hours of the morning—weary travelers breaking up a long trip, waitresses ending their day, cops starting theirs. I'd sit half-awake in the claustrophobic kiosk of the station that consisted of two tiny rooms and an even smaller washroom that could barely fit a toilet and sink. I spent my shifts swiping credit cards, giving change, and occasionally giving directions to drivers who were lost.

Just before midnight one night, I started a shift as my best friend, who also worked there, ended hers. As I stood behind the sliding pane of glass in the kiosk, waiting for my first customer, a man entered the station wearing a dark ski mask. He pointed a gun directly at my face. "Open the door!" he yelled. My heart raced. I was paralyzed by fear, my eyes bulging out of my head like I was a cartoon character.

He motioned with his gun toward the kiosk door and thundered obscenities as he yelled again, "Open the door!" From the corner of my eye, I could see another masked gunman by that door, impatiently waiting for me to unlock it.

Instead of obeying his instruction, I panicked. I let out a blood-curdling scream and dove headfirst for safety into the adjoining room where the cash was locked up. I think I scared him even more than he scared me.

Preoccupied, my friend hadn't heard the raving gunman but was startled by my piercing scream and hard landing. "What's your problem?" she shrieked. She turned her head toward the direction I had just flown out of and saw the gunmen. As the guy by the door yelled at her to open it, she too panicked—and opened the door for him.

Both men shoved their way into the kiosk. One made his way toward me, his steel-toed boots heavily pounding on the floor. As he dragged me into the washroom, I could hear his buddy yell at my friend, "Put the money in the bag! And some cigarettes too!"

My gunman whipped out a long piece of rope and started wrapping it around my wrists. I sat on the floor in an awkward position. "Don't do anything stupid," he warned. Slamming the washroom door shut, he left me alone in the dark. I felt a mixture of fear and the chill of the toilet tank pressed against my face. I shivered, listening to the gunmen order my friend around and her whimpers to please not hurt her. I almost didn't believe what was happening. *Are they going to hurt us? Kill us? Is this even real?*

Then as quickly as it began, the robbery ended. The men left with thousands of dollars and a pillowcase-sized bag full of cartons of cigarettes. Less than five minutes after the gunmen forced their way in, my best friend stumbled into the washroom to get me. Her hands shook like a bowlful of jelly as she untied the rope around my wrists. We dialed the police and waited in fear, hoping to God that the gunmen wouldn't be back. It was the last day I'd ever work there. There was no way I was risking another robbery or something even worse.

Without the gas station job, my money quickly ran dry. Soon I was broke, trying to maintain a high party lifestyle and still pay rent. I had to figure out a way to make money somehow. Ironically, I began to steal cigarettes from a low-end chain store. I'd walk in the store, grab a few cartons, hide them under my puffy Starter jacket, and walk out the front door. No one suspected me. My jacket was so huge, I could easily fit four cartons underneath that oversized thing. A pack of cigarettes cost about eight bucks back then, and I sold the entire ten-pack carton for twenty-five. It was a steal (pun intended), but it still wasn't enough to pay for my partying expenses.

So I started dealing pot. Other people were doing it at school and making a ton of money. It was quick and easy, and because I looked so young and clean-cut, I was the least suspicious drug dealer you could find. It's a miracle I never got caught. I could have gone to jail.

In the big picture, the consequences could have been a lot worse for me. I could have ended up robbing gas stations myself, or addicted to powerful drugs like meth. I'm certainly not trying to be the poster child for a recovering drug addict. I'm thankful I didn't have to go through the painful process of recovering from substance abuse.

I eventually moved back home after a few months on my own. The fighting between my mom and me picked up right where it left off. I feel terrible for what I put my mother through when I was a teenager. I threw all the anger and pain that had built up in me all those years at her. I didn't know how to deal with the wrestling match in my soul—hating myself one minute, wanting to be loved the next; full of rage one minute, not caring about anything the next. I'm embarrassed when I think about how rebellious I was at home, but it also makes me sad because it came from a place of deep pain. I always say those who are hardest to love need it the most.

Around the same time, I also fell back into my familiar pattern with Jeremy. We reignited our toxic relationship. Jeremy and I hung out a lot with our mutual friends, either partying or doing stupid things.

One time, when I was almost seventeen, we were hanging out with our group of equally trouble-making friends. It was evening but still light outside, and like usual, we were broke and bored. We were loitering around the downtown area when we found an unlocked building. (Is it breaking and entering if the door is open?)

The empty warehouse was huge and for the most part empty. We scattered around the room, nosily going through closets and cup-

> Sometimes teenagers do bad things because they are crying out for attention. They may be hurt, depressed, or struggling with emotional problems. If you know someone who is engaging in destructive behaviors, talk to them or tell an adult you trust. It's hard to ask for help, but by reaching out you can make a difference to someone who needs it.

boards to find, well, something. We found a bunch of yoga mats and dragged them to the open floor where we had a mini Olympic session complete with sloppy cartwheels and lopsided handsprings. Yeah, we weren't jocks.

After a while gymnastics got boring, so we started sneaking around the building. Still in the semi-dark, someone opened a massive cupboard that revealed a staircase. It was the strangest thing, finding a staircase in a cupboard. We started imagining the horrible things we would find at the bottom of the stairs, until one of the guys dared another to be a man and check it out.

One tough guy accepted the challenge. He opened the door and slowly moved down a couple of steps farther into total darkness, but then he freaked out and ran back up. Poor thing. We couldn't help but tease him.

Another guy piped up at that point. With his chest puffed out he said arrogantly, "I'll do it." He didn't even make it halfway down the stairs before he too got spooked and ran back up.

I thought the whole thing was silly. I mean, seriously, what on earth could we possibly find down there? I straightened up all of my four-foot-six bad self, said, "This is a job for a real woman," and marched down the staircase. I groped my hand around on the wall, feeling for a light switch, and when I finally found one, I couldn't believe what I saw.

I gasped. When my voice echoed up the stairs, my friends started freaking out and ran away from the door. "No, wait!" I shouted. "You guys gotta come down here. This is awesome! You're not gonna believe this!" Though hesitant, my friends made their way down.

"Whoa," someone said as they all reached the bottom and looked around. "This is unreal."

We all stood paralyzed with disbelief in the middle of a giant room that was the equivalent of a teenagers' playground. Video games, basketball hoops, a jukebox, and dartboards were all around us. It was like we found ourselves in a whole new world. Then it hit me. This must be the community center called the Bunker that I had read about in the local paper. We'd found it before it even opened. It was a proud moment for all of us.

For the next few hours, we were in heaven. The arcade games were open so you could put in a quarter, play a game, and get your money back to keep playing. We played game after game. We shot hoops. We blasted tunes on the jukebox. We played pool and Ping-Pong. And then we got bored.

I started snooping around and noticed a booth in the corner that was locked. There had to be some money in there, or at least some snacks. As we huddled around the lock, trying to shake the thing open, we heard an indistinct noise on the other side of the building. We froze. Someone was there. Once we heard a door open and slam shut at an entrance other than where we had come in, we knew we had to get out of there. Fast. With our adrenaline pumping and nervous laughter, we booked it out of the building the same way we came in.

Because we found the place before opening day, we proudly hailed it as "ours." That seal of ownership was the only reason we ever went back. It was a Christian place, after all. There were Bible verses all over the walls and a cheesy sign that said, "No Drinking. No Smoking. No Swearing."

Right.

When the Bunker opened to the public, we were there every weekend. It gave us something to do and a place to go. When I didn't feel like playing a video game or shooting pool, I'd hang out with John Brown, the director of the center. I'll never forget the mullet hairstyle he wore for a long time, all business in the front and party in the back. He looked like he was stuck in the eighties. I'd always tell him, "Hey, John, the eighties called. They want their hair back." Though I wasn't a fan of his hairstyle, I found him so easy to talk to. He was caring and sincere, and no matter how hard I tried, I couldn't find an ulterior motive behind his goodness. We had a lot of deep talks about life.

There was only one thing about him that bothered me. He talked about God. A lot. No matter what we talked about, he would always find a way to bring the conversation back to God. It was annoying. But I let him ramble on and on about religious stuff because he was nice. And the truth was, I really liked him.

Even though John was kind to Jeremy, my friends, and me, he wasn't clueless to what we were doing. If he caught us breaking the rules, he kicked us out of the center immediately, although of course he always let us back in the next weekend.

John was the first person who gave me a chance. Who didn't dismiss me because I was young, stupid, or a troublemaker. He was someone who listened. And truly cared. As the "father figure" of the youth center, he had a kindness and integrity I was drawn to. He always encouraged my friends and me to do the right thing.

One weekend in May of 1992, my friends and I celebrated May Two-Four (Victoria Day), a Canadian holiday celebrating Queen Victoria's birthday. It's a big party weekend. Jeremy and I had broken up a week earlier after I found out he'd cheated on me. The getaway was my escape—a chance to go camping, hang out with my friends, let loose, and leave my relationship drama at home.

> Sometimes we are so hurt and broken that we look for love in things, people, or places that ultimately hurt us. Instead of filling that void in an unhealthy way, we need to figure out how to become healthy on our own.

I drank too much and hooked up with a guy I knew from school. It was dumb and I regretted it immediately. A few days later, Jeremy called, and we performed the same old song and dance routine. He apologized for breaking my heart and begged me to take him back. He was saying all the right things, all the things he knew could turn me into a deep pile of mush. "Baby, I love you." "Please come back to me." "I'll change." "I can't live without you." "We're so good for each other." "You're the only one I want." I was hopelessly defenseless. Of course I would do my part and take him back. I did every time.

I figured, though, that I needed to be honest with him about what had happened on my weekend away. So I confessed what I had done.

Big mistake.

At first, Jeremy was quiet. It didn't take long, however, for chaos to break out. As I tried to choke back tears and pleaded with him to calm down, Jeremy went nuts. All I could hear was pounding fists, heavy objects crashing, and glass shattering.

I felt terrible. Guilty and ashamed. Especially because his rage was sparked by a foolish choice I made. Still holding the phone to my ear and listening to Jeremy's screams in the background, I got dizzy from all the emotions that swirled in my head.

I knew at some point, he'd calm down. I'd say I was sorry a million times, he'd throw in a few more digs, and we'd eventually kiss and make up (only to do a repeat a few weeks later).

But this time was different. Jeremy threatened to expose my darkest secrets—things I'd shared with him a few weeks earlier in a moment of vulnerability. In hindsight, I can see that everything Jeremy said came from a place of deep hurt. But in that moment all I could hear was a threat that cut to the deepest part of me.

All I felt was darkness. Pure, utter darkness.

The phone dropped from my hand as if in slow motion and landed with a thud. Life as I knew it stopped. The world turned black. I couldn't breathe.

My hands started shaking, and all I could hear was the gasps coming from my throat as I struggled for oxygen. As his words echoed in my head, a wave of shame drowned my logic, and in that moment all I could think was, *I have to die.* And it had to happen now.

In a matter of minutes, I closed the gap between wanting to die and trying to die. But how would I do it? I thought of my sister and how she was killed.

Bingo.

I walked outside the house and waited for the perfect opportunity. It had to be a truck. A big one. I didn't want to allow for any

"Suicide accounts for about 4,400 deaths annually among 10- to 24-year-olds. . . . Among high school students, 15 percent report having seriously considered suicide in the past year, 11 percent created a suicide plan and 7 percent attempted suicide."

National Conference of State Legislators[7]

miscalculations. I'd time my death perfectly, I thought. I watched as cars whizzed by on my street. Chevy Impala? Too small. Ford Escort? Even smaller. Minivan? Getting there. Then I caught a glimpse of an oncoming box truck. Perfect.

Adrenaline pumped in my veins like a percussion solo. As the truck got closer, I ran toward the street, across our square front lawn and the cracked sidewalk where I used to play hopscotch. A few strides farther, and I jumped off the curb directly into the truck's path. Midair, I could make out the face of the driver, who was turning white as a ghost.

> Suicide is the third leading cause of death of people ages 15 to 24. It's also the fourth leading cause of death for children under 14.[8]

I closed my eyes and expected to be pummeled to the ground by the moving weight of this massive vehicle. But nothing happened. The driver slammed on his brakes and adeptly maneuvered the skidding truck onto a side street right in front of my house. He missed. He was probably thanking God in that moment. I was cursing Him.

The screeching brakes pierced my ears. I was alive, with skinned knees and a few bruises to boot. I felt devastated and humiliated that I couldn't even end my own life. I saw the truck driver run toward me, sweat pouring down the sides of his face. Poor guy. I had given him the scare of his life.

"Are you all right?" he panted, out of breath and showing genuine concern.

I was speechless. Numb. I merely nodded in a haze and turned toward my house. My eyes were met by a fuming neighbor who had watched me attempt to kill myself. She looked at me with such anger, as if I had just killed her best friend. I certainly didn't expect what came next.

She screamed obscenities at me from her porch and then came running in my direction, her eyes bulging with poison. When she got an arm's length away, she grabbed me, dragged me, and whipped me up onto my porch. As she cursed and called me terrible names, she spat with anger, "How could you do this? What were you thinking? How could you be so selfish?"

I floated in and out of my thoughts as my neighbor continued her mean screamfest. Frankly, I didn't see the point. I was quite the expert at calling me names and putting me down. There was no need for her to gut my heart like a fish. I did a fantastic job on my own, thank you very much. What I really needed in that moment was compassion.

As I curled up in a fetal position, drowning out the neighbor's voice with my own thoughts, she finally threw her hands up in surrender. My stepbrother showed up on the porch, his eyes wide in shock, and my neighbor handed me off to him.

Chuck led me inside the house and asked, "What happened? What made you do this?"

The living room spun out of control and my mind was far away, far from the table in the corner, the old-fashioned couches, my stepbrother's face close to mine as he played detective to figure out what just happened and why. He called my mom at some point. As we waited for her to show up, Chuck continued to ask me questions.

"Talk to me, Pattie. What got you to this point?" he asked again, determined to get me to talk.

I couldn't say a word. I was frozen. Trapped. I just sat at the kitchen table, stuffing my anger inside, and numbly stared out into space. I knew my mom would be home soon. What on earth would I say to her? As I sat on the cold, hard chair, I couldn't escape the gnawing feeling of wanting to die.

Suicide attempts are a cry for help. They are not a joke. Take them seriously. People who try to kill themselves are hurting on such a deep level. Don't look down on the person or call him or her crazy. Show that you care and want to help.

If you or someone you know is contemplating suicide, talk to your parents or a trusted adult immediately. You can also contact the following groups to get help or for more information.

- National Suicide Prevention Lifeline: 1-800-273-8255
- American Foundation for Suicide Prevention: http://www.afsp.org
- The Society for the Prevention of Teen Suicide: http://www.sptsusa.org

It was all I could think about. It wasn't a loud thought. It was soft, a mere whisper. *Die, Pattie. Just die.* The soothing lullaby hypnotized me.

When my mom came home and sat at the table with me, her hands shaky as she tried to compose herself as much as possible, I opened up. I blurted out the truth of all I had suffered and told her about how I had been repeatedly abused for five years by those we both knew. I told her how I had agonized in shame and in secret for years. I told her I couldn't handle it. And I didn't know what to do with the pain.

I saw my mother soften a bit. And after we sat in silence for a few seconds, she made a shocking admission. "Stuff happened to me too, when I was young." She didn't say much after that. She didn't need to.

I don't think either one of us knew what to do at that point.

It was my mom who broke the silence. "I'm taking you to the hospital. We're going to get you help."

five

I am troubled
I feel empty
I don't know what I want
Comfort, love and mostly attention
I have a wall built around my heart
I am worried
I am sad
And I'm filled with regret
Regret for not saying no
When I was little
When I was curious
And when I was hopeful

I wrote this poem on May 20, 1992, the day before I was admitted to Stratford General Hospital.

The evidence that I needed help was there all along. Silent cries. Depression. Acting out. Rebellion. All signs I was fighting for attention, for someone to stop and listen and tell me I mattered. Like so many others, I suffered in silence, unsure of how to claw my way out of despair and into light. The only way I knew how was to kill myself.

It hadn't been the first time I'd wanted to do so. Almost two years earlier to the day, I had written in my journal, "I'm so depressed lately. I'm always crying, and I've thought about suicide a couple of times but I doubt I'd ever get enough stupidness to do it." I guess I'd finally found the "stupidness."

I didn't protest my mom's suggestion of going to the hospital; a part of me felt I had to go. I was just embarrassed. I was a patient for nineteen days, much longer than I would have guessed.

I want to get one thing straight, though. The psych ward was nothing like what you see in the movies. The floor wasn't a human zoo filled with patients wetting their pants and being chased by orderlies. I didn't see people in zombie-like trances aimlessly walking the hallways, talking to themselves. The ward was actually quiet. And very sad.

> If you have suicidal thoughts, don't be ashamed to get help. It's not a sign of weakness. Talking to someone shows that you care enough about yourself to want to get better.

My roommate was there because she tried to kill herself by taking a bunch of pills. She seemed normal, friendly, and polite. Just like me. But if you paid enough attention to her beautiful face, you could make out a glaze over her distant eyes. I guess it's easy to recognize the look when you see it every day in the mirror.

I didn't think I was all that different from the other patients. We had a bond; we were all troubled, just to different degrees and in different ways. Each of us was there to ultimately try to make sense out of our messes. Whether it was finding a reason to live, or figuring out why we hated ourselves so much, or, like me, trying to get to the bottom of an unmanageable depression.

> You can be on the lookout for friends or peers who are at risk for committing suicide. Here are some signs:
>
> - Frequently talking about death/suicide
> - Making a suicide plan
> - Thinking nobody cares about him or her
> - Major changes in personality and behavior
> - Destructive, aggressive, and reckless behaviors
> - Withdrawal from friends and family
> - Severe depression
> - Spending time researching or socializing with people who glamorize suicide

Why did I throw myself in front of a truck? Why did I keep returning to a volatile relationship? Why did I think ending my life was better than living it? I had a ton of questions—some obvious, others unknown—that needed to be investigated. A big part of me was ready to talk about my past. But I didn't get to do that in the hospital.

It wasn't until a few years ago that I finally had the opportunity to bring about lasting healing by dealing with the abuse. But back at the hospital as a teenager, I felt like none of the reasons I found myself in a psych ward, specifically the aftermath of the many years I had been sexually abused, were any more than merely mentioned in passing.

I was lonely in the hospital. There wasn't much to do outside of popping meds, watching TV, going to group therapy, and hanging out in the common area. I felt trapped, like I'd been given a prison sentence without the possibility of parole. None of the therapy seemed to be working. I was the same person with the same depressing thoughts, low self-esteem, and haunting past.

I didn't even get many visitors. Outside of my parents and John Brown, the director of the Bunker, I don't remember anyone stopping by. It was a sobering wake-up call that I had no real friends. Sure, I had plenty who would party with me in an instant, but when I hit rock bottom, none of my party buddies showed up.

> Teens who are depressed or struggling emotionally turn to their friends or peers before their parents. You can be a positive influence on someone who may need help. Be kind, encouraging, and supportive to others. A small act of kindness goes a long way.

John, on the other hand, was determined to show me he was genuine and he really did care. He regularly visited with me. I always knew he was coming because I could smell him from down the hallway. Well, not him exactly, but rather the unmistakable, mouthwatering aroma of the fast food he brought. John would walk into my room carrying greasy bags of McDonald's and KFC, and my eyes would immediately light up.

I didn't mind John's visits so much, even though he droned on and on about God. Though I was used to his constant God-babble from hanging out with him at the youth center, at times it got annoying. *God this. God that.* As I half-listened while munching on french fries and fried chicken, I remember thinking, "This guy can't stop talking about God, and it's not even Sunday." Needless to say, he still left quite an impression.

The first time John came to visit, he brought a rose and told me that God told him to tell me He loved me and saw me like that rose—beautiful. I chewed on a Big Mac and stared at the perfect flower. First of all, I thought John was nuts for telling me he heard from God. Second, I thought he was completely off his rocker when God's message was that I was as beautiful as the flower John was holding.

Somehow I was able to get past the whole hearing-from-God bit. But I just couldn't escape the comparison to the rose. *Oh my gosh, there is no way I'm like that rose. I'm not beautiful. I'm not good. I feel dirty, ashamed, and guilty because of the poor choices I've made. The sleeping around. The drinking. The stealing. The drugs. Beautiful? What planet is this guy on?* John continued to visit me and to share God's love for me in a caring way, but the more he talked, the more I thought he had gone bonkers. What did he know about God's love for me? Obviously not much.

One day he said something that struck me, something I couldn't even roll my eyes at in my head. "Pattie, when you hit rock bottom, you have nowhere to go but up. You don't want to live anyway, so why don't you just see what God can do with your life and what plans He has for you?"

With eyes of compassion John asked, "What do you have to lose?"

Though we'd had many heart-to-hearts about God, I'd never even entertained John's passionate belief that God loved me. I'd never experienced God before, let

> *"Pattie, when you hit rock bottom, you have nowhere to go but up. You don't want to live anyway, so why don't you just see what God can do with your life and what plans He has for you?"*

alone the kind of love John shared with me. Frankly, at that point in my life, I didn't know if I believed God even existed.

What do you have to lose?

The question stumped me. I was speechless because the truth was, John was right. I had nothing to lose. I had tried doing life my way and failed miserably.

After John left that day, his words echoed in my head. As I lay in bed, plagued by my life choices, by the path I had chosen, and by my painful childhood, I realized I really didn't have a better option.

I lay there feeling vulnerable. What was I going to say? Either I was about to pray to the God of the universe, or I would be talking to the ceiling like a lunatic. "Um, God," I began. "If You're real, I pray You do what John said. Help me live my life. I don't know how to do this on my own." A part of me wondered what God could possibly do with my life. But I saw it as the ultimate challenge. I'd see what, if anything, He could do to rewrite the story I had so poorly written myself. I was willing to give it a shot.

> It doesn't matter what you've done or what has happened to you. There is always hope. Things can get better. You can change. No matter how bad your problems, there is a better future in store for you. Trust God to help you find your way.

I knew there was more I had to say. I couldn't just stop there. John had talked to me before about how we are all sinners and how our sin separates us from God. He sent His Son, Jesus, to die for our sins so that if we accept His forgiveness, we will be reconciled to God. So I asked Jesus, "Would You forgive me of all my sins?"

The moment I said those words, vivid images flashed across my mind. I'm sure you've heard stories of how when people are about to die, they see their lives flash before their eyes. Well, that's exactly like what happened to me, except what I saw wasn't very pleasant. Every sin, every wrong, every bad choice—everything I had done that was against what God desired for my life came to my mind. The drugs. The drinking. The stealing. I couldn't see how God could even begin to forgive me. Maybe I had gone too far, done too much.

I felt so ashamed. I took my eyes off the ceiling, looked down at my hospital-issued slippers, and whispered, "If it's too late, God, I totally understand."

But then He showed up. God met me in such a powerful way, there was no way I could doubt His existence or His presence anymore.

Pardon the cheesy-sounding details, but what I experienced next was very intense and very real. With my eyes closed, I saw in my mind an image of my heart opening up. As it unfolded, gold dust was poured into the opening and filled every inch of my heart until there was no room left for even one more speck to squeeze through. Somehow deep in my spirit I knew the gold dust represented God's love; He was pouring His love into my heart. Then as quickly as it filled up, my heart closed and turned a blindingly bright white. I felt like I had been cleansed from the inside out. I was in awe, and I was fully aware of God's presence.

But here's the thing: I didn't feel loved in a warm and fuzzy way. It was like a deep knowing. A love that could only come from God.

I started crying. Tears of relief. Tears of hope. Tears of gratitude. I had just found Someone I had been looking for all my life. Still trying to wrap my brain around what had just happened, I sat in a daze, uttering in wide-eyed amazement,

"Oh my God . . . YOU are real."

"Oh my GOD . . . You ARE real."

"OH MY GOD . . . You are REAL!"

"Oh my God . . . You're really real!"

For the next few minutes, I sat unable to move. I was so overwhelmed by this knowing, all I could do was repeat that God was real.

> *"Do you think anyone is going to be able to drive a wedge between us and Christ's love for us? There is no way! Not trouble, not hard times, not hatred, not hunger, not homelessness, not bullying threats, not backstabbing, not even the worst sins. . . . Absolutely nothing can get between us and God's love."*
>
> (Romans 8:35, 39 in *The Message*)

I knew that if I was going to give God control of my life, there were certain things I would have to give up. If there was anything I understood about God from the little I had learned from John and my minimal Catholic background, it was that God didn't approve of certain things. Mainly, the things I liked to do.

> God isn't a mean schoolteacher on a power trip who demands we follow rules "just because" or a Santa Claus who weighs whether we've been bad or good. There are certain things we shouldn't do because they're bad for us and in the end will cause more harm than good.

So believe it or not, I took a deep breath and gave God an ultimatum. "God, if I have to give up my drugs and my alcohol, You'd better be better than them, because I like drinking and I like my drugs. But here's the thing: I'm not gonna play church. I'm not gonna be a pew warmer and be a pretend Christian or a hypocrite. So I'll give that stuff up, but You'd better be worth it." Maybe it wasn't the most reverent prayer, but it was honest. It was where my heart was. I've come to realize that God loves for us to be raw and real with Him.

I sat up and opened the drawer of the nightstand by my hospital bed. I reached in and found a Bible. Somehow I just knew I had to start reading it. It was my first time, and I wasn't sure where or how to begin; I just opened it up to a random page and started reading.

I didn't know a thing about the Bible. I certainly didn't know there were different versions of the book. The one I had in my hand was a King James Version, probably not the most reader-friendly for a newbie teenage believer. It was a black-and-white blur. All I could make out was "thee this" and "thou that," "art this" and "ye that." Every other word sounded like something from a foreign language or a Shakespearean play. I guessed God had a different way of speaking than normal people like me. "Okay, God," I piped up. "If I'm going to do this thing, You're going to have to teach me Your language."

———————

I was so excited about what I had just experienced, I ran to the pay phone (do pay phones even exist anymore?) down the hall to call John. He was the only person I knew who would appreciate what I had just gone through. And maybe he could help me understand God's language. I thought about the many times he had talked to me about God and how what he shared had meant nothing to me. But after my encounter with God, everything John had said and tried to teach me came alive.

By the time I got to the phone and dialed John's number, I was out of breath from excitement. "You are not going to believe this," I blurted out.

"What's the matter?" He sounded concerned.

"Are you sitting down?"

"Yeah, sure, Pattie. What's wrong?" God only knows what John was thinking at this point.

"GOD IS REAL!" I practically shouted in his ear. I waited for John to react in a dramatic, almost disbelieving way. I expected him to say, "No way! C'mon! Get out of town!" After all, I thought I was telling him something he didn't already know, something that would turn his world upside down like it had mine. I knew John was a Christian, but I didn't think he knew the truth like I did. After all, *I* had just had an experience with God.

John laughed and was clearly enjoying the moment. I wasn't. I was getting irritated. *I can't believe this! He's not getting it.* I tried again, repeating what I had just said, this time drawing out the words more. "GOD"—long pause—"IS REAL!"

"Yes, I know," John said patiently and by this point, I'm guessing, with a grin from ear to ear.

"No, no, no. You don't understand. I just had an experience. I'm not talking about the religion stuff you learn in church. I'm talking about the real deal." I continued passionately stating my case. "The God of the universe, the God who created you and me and the skies and the trees—John, that God is real!"

"Yes, I know. That's what I've been trying to tell you."

"Oh. Well, I just tried to read the Bible, but I can't understand it. It's full of thees and thous and says things like 'heretofore, inasmuch, wherewithal, notwithstanding.' And I don't understand a word of it. You're gonna have to teach me God's language."

"That's not God's language," John explained as he chuckled. "That's King James's language. The original Bible was written in Greek and Hebrew and later translated into English. So the King James Version is an Old English version."

John told me he'd be right over with a Bible I'd have an easier time reading. That evening in the hospital room, he prayed with me and read the Bible with me, a version in today's language I could understand.

John was so happy for me. And I am so thankful for him because he taught me what it means to be a real Christian through the example he lived day in and day out. This wonderful man helped me to learn what God's love and grace is all about.

Before I was discharged from the hospital a week later, my doctors couldn't help but notice the change in my attitude. I told them about my encounter with God and that He was real.

They were suspicious. "So you're hearing voices now?" one of them asked me.

No, I wasn't hearing voices! I had met God. And I wasn't depressed anymore. I felt alive. I had found purpose. For the first time in my life, I felt free. I could think clearly. I felt a deep, indescribable love, a love that was the perfect fit for the hole in my heart that nothing in the past was ever able to fill.

After I got out of the hospital, I was on a natural high for about a week. I was finally fulfilled and didn't feel the need to use drugs, alcohol, or even unhealthy relationships to self-medicate, forget, or feel wanted. I had found what I didn't even know had been missing in my life.

At the time, Jeremy wasn't the biggest fan of my new faith. Maybe he felt threatened because he didn't have the same power over me as he'd had before. And for the first time, I could see how toxic and volatile our relationship was.

Jeremy came to visit me one afternoon and I told him about my new life change. While he wanted us to start dating again, I didn't think it was a good idea. He told me all the reasons that we should get back together. I wasn't convinced and instead told him about God. Jeremy, however, didn't think much about my new faith and left.

My spiritual high naturally went away. At some point you've got to come out of the clouds and live real life. I couldn't live forever on blissful feelings. I had to learn to balance the high with the realities of life.

Though I was traveling down a new path of hope, I still had a lot of problems I needed to work on. The trauma I endured from my past sexual abuse and the harmful thought patterns I developed as a result weren't going to go away on their own or in an instant. Healing would come, but only over time and in bits and pieces. Unfortunately, I didn't understand that then. And that's why I ultimately returned to the very things that had led me to my breaking point.

When I got out of the hospital, I started going to a nondenominational church that was different from what I had imagined church was like. Though no church is perfect and you'll find hypocrites in every one, for the most part, I found the Christians at the church I attended to be very real and authentic. They actually walked the walk and talked the talk. They led me by their example.

My hunger to know everything about my newfound faith was insatiable. For the next six months, I faithfully attended church every Sunday, sitting in the front row week after week. I went to

Bible study. I was mentored by different leaders. I read books. I even called the pastors at all hours of the day and night (sorry about that, guys!) to ask questions and ask for prayer. I was a spiritual sponge.

The more knowledge I soaked up, the more I distanced myself from my partying friends. I didn't think I was better than them because my life was changing in a different way; we just didn't share much in common anymore. I didn't want to spend nights and weekends partying. I wanted to clean up my act. I didn't want to depend on drugs, alcohol, or guys to make me feel better anymore. Little by little the friendships I had made, mainly through partying and getting wasted, started fading away.

> Christianity isn't the end of all problems. It's the beginning of learning dependence on Jesus Christ. We become transformed when we exchange what we think of ourselves for what God thinks about us.

A few months after my encounter with God, though, I found myself frustrated because certain issues I struggled with weren't going away. I thought that after experiencing a second chance at life, I'd turn into a totally different person. I thought my bad habits would just go away. I thought I would automatically become this perfect person who always did the right thing, never got angry, and had no leftover pain from her past. But that's not what happened.

Thing is, the faith life isn't about being perfect. Change takes time. It doesn't happen overnight. It's a continual process. I had some work to do in my inner life, but at the time I didn't realize it would be a gradual thing.

I also felt alone. While I was fortunate to have so many people in the church to love and teach me, they were all much older. They had spouses and families of their own to take care of. I wanted—really I needed—to hang out with kids I could relate to and talk

I know it's hard not fitting in, especially when you're lonely. But don't sell out yourself or your morals or make dumb decisions just to be part of a crowd. It's never worth it. Following the crowd doesn't mean they're going in the right direction. You need to do what's right, and the joy will follow.

to about school, music, and your average teenage stuff. I needed friends my own age.

A few months after getting out of the hospital, I made a slow but deliberate detour. A few steps backward here and a few more there, and before I knew it, I was back at parties, doing all the bad things I used to do.

I didn't intend to go back to my old partying ways, but John had warned me it could happen. Though I swore that I would be a good influence on my friends—he knew better.

"Let me put it this way," he told me as he slid a chair out from his desk during one of our many mentoring meetings. "Stand on this chair."

I did.

John reached out his hand. "Now take my hand."

Almost immediately after I grabbed his hand, his strong grip pulled me down.

"Think about it. Is it easier for you to pull me up or for me to pull you down?"

Point taken.

But his illustration didn't stop me from visiting my old turf. I started going back to parties. Not drinking at first, just hanging out with old friends my age. It was only a short matter of time before I

The right thing to do is often the hardest thing to do.

started compromising a little here, a little there. Then I was back to drinking and doing drugs.

I stopped going to church as often and had fewer conversations with John and other leaders at the church. While I didn't give up on God, the pull toward the past was too strong. The old bad habits and desires came back full force. But it wasn't the same. The difference was I felt guilty. And I couldn't escape that feeling. A year after I tried to kill myself, the peace and joy I'd once had was gone and replaced with waves of guilt. I was no dummy. I knew I wasn't living right. I knew I wasn't supposed to be doing the things I was doing.

I wanted to pray, but I had a hard time. Words didn't come easily. I didn't know what to say. Feeling too far away from God, I made matters worse. I dug deeper into my old ways. As the final straw, I got back together with Jeremy. I hadn't seen him in a while, but he wanted to hang out on his birthday. I said yes.

Two weeks later, I was at the gynecologist's office. It was the last place I wanted to be. I could think of a thousand different things I would have rather been doing. Getting a root canal sounded better. I wouldn't have even minded being grounded.

It was supposed to be a routine visit, but the checkup took longer than I had expected. I watched the hands of the clock on the wall creep agonizingly forward as my mom sat in the corner, her face buried in a tabloid magazine.

The doctor snapped off his latex gloves, whipped them into a nearby trash can, and without missing a beat said, "Any chance you could be pregnant?"

My mom's magazine fell to the floor, the pages fluttering noisily about.

Are you kidding me?

The doctor asked me again, with the same casual beat he'd use to ask me if it was raining, "Is it possible you could be pregnant?"

I know it may sound crazy or old-fashioned, but sex before marriage is never a good thing. Many consequences can come as a result, including:

- sexually transmitted diseases (STDs) and infections (STIs)
- lower academic achievement
- teen pregnancy
- out-of-wedlock childbearing
- and let's not forget: possibly feeling used and ending up with a broken heart

Want to avoid these risks? Abstain from sexual activity.

I immediately looked at my mom, who sat in stunned silence, and loudly retorted, "No! Absolutely not! No way!" My face was beet red. I was embarrassed but also offended. How dare this doctor ask me if I'm pregnant in front of my mother! Couldn't he have pulled me aside? Asked my mother to leave the room? Called me the next day?

I sat up on the table and pulled my paper gown protectively around me. Pregnant? "There's no way I'm pregnant, doctor," I repeated resolutely.

"I don't know what to tell you, Pattie." The doctor shrugged. "From what I could tell, I'm pretty sure you are, so . . ." He started writing on a prescription pad. "I'm sending you to the clinic next door to get a pregnancy test." He ripped off the piece of paper and put it in my hand, annoyed.

My mother let out a muffled groan. "Dear God, Pattie, please don't tell me you're pregnant."

I rolled my eyes at both of them. "I'm not pregnant!"

I wasn't pregnant. I couldn't be. It was impossible. After all, I was taking birth control pills.

Nevertheless, my mother and I walked to the clinic next door. Neither of us said a word. My mom probably didn't see any point

Sexually transmitted infections and diseases are a serious problem.

- Though 1 in 5 Americans has genital herpes, nearly 90 percent are unaware they have it. Some estimates suggest that by 2025 up to 40 percent of all men and half of all women could be infected.[9]
- Nearly 9 million young people are infected with sexually transmitted infections every year.[10]
- Many sexually transmitted diseases, including HIV, can be transmitted through oral sex.[11]
- A girl is four times more likely to contract an STI/STD than she is to become pregnant.[12]

in questioning me again. We'd find out the truth in a matter of minutes. I stared at the cheesy posters on the wall in the waiting room. One told me to exercise regularly. Another reminded me to eat more fruits and vegetables. The walls looked muddied. Dim and dirty. *Why am I here?* I wanted to run out of the room and not look back.

"Pattie Mallette?" A nurse's head peeked through a half-open door into the room. "You can come in now."

I was still in denial. Doctor, nurse, whatever—no one was going to tell me I was pregnant.

After another test and a few more minutes of waiting, I stood in another room, having offered the only chair available to my mom. She probably needed it more than me. She looked like she was going to faint at any moment.

The door opened and the same nurse who had performed my test came in. She nodded sympathetically and said, "Pattie, the doctor was right. You are pregnant."

In the background I heard my mother say faintly, almost in a whisper, "Oh, Pattie." Her voice was soft, but I could hear the disappointment loud and clear. Absolute and utter disappointment.

I almost lost it. *Lies, these are all lies.* I looked at the nurse like she needed to get her head examined. "No way. There is no way I'm pregnant. You're gonna have to do it again. The test is wrong."

The nurse repeated more firmly, "Pattie, you're pregnant. The test is 99.9 percent accurate."

I didn't budge. "Well, then there's still a chance I'm not pregnant. Do it again."

At my prompting, she did another test.

While waiting the second time, I started doubting myself. I started to entertain the maybes. When the nurse came back, she repeated her earlier diagnosis. I had no more wiggle room to deny the obvious. I was going to have a baby.

I was leaning against a wall when the nurse told me the results from the second test. I crumpled down to the ground like a rag doll. I was in shock. Overwhelmed. A baby? Now? The timing couldn't have been any worse.

I wasn't married. I wasn't old enough. I wasn't responsible. I was back sowing my old wild oats. A baby didn't fit anywhere in that picture. A baby didn't even belong near that picture.

I had nothing against children. I loved kids. I'd always wanted to have babies. But I had romantic hopes around that dream. I would have a husband. A handsome, supportive, loving husband. And a beautiful home with a white picket fence and maybe even a dog.

> "Some 67% of teen girls and 53% of teen boys who have had sex wish they had waited longer.
>
> "Nine in 10 teens (91%) say they want to be married before they have/father a child."
>
> The National Campaign to Prevent Teen and Unplanned Pregnancies[13]

But a baby in my life situation? Half praying, half crying, I sobbed, "Oh, God, no, no, no! What am I going to do?"

While I continued my emotional outburst, my mom was quiet. She comforted me as best as she could by reassuringly patting my shoulder.

Finding out you're pregnant as an unwed teenager brings with it a flurry of emotions. You may feel shocked, ashamed, guilty, or worried. It's especially difficult to make the life-changing decision that will determine your baby's future (and yours)—whether to be a single parent or consider adoption.

Talk to trusted and supportive adults and mentors like your parents, a teacher, a pastor, or a youth leader. Or you can find a pregnancy crisis center near you, like I did. There are plenty of resources out there.

Consider your financial resources, your level of commitment, and the consequences of your choice. Ask yourself if you can live with your decision without regret. Also, do your homework. Contact local adoption agencies and research your options.

Don't rush into any decision. Take your time. Think it through. Be as informed as you can to make the best decision for your baby.

I stumbled around for days, disoriented and still in shock. I couldn't process the reality—in less than nine months, I'd be the mother of a flesh and blood, living and breathing baby. It was a dream, right? And I was going to wake up real soon?

My mom made it clear that raising the baby would be my responsibility, not hers. I knew I'd be on my own and had some difficult decisions to make. I made the choice to keep my baby and not have an abortion. It was ironic considering that when I was on the high school debate team, I made many convincing arguments for a woman's right to choose.

Honestly, I was shocked at the pressure put on me to have an abortion. I just didn't feel it was right for me to do. I also didn't think I had the emotional strength to place my child for adoption. I wanted my baby.

I took matters into my own hands and started researching a bunch of pregnancy centers from the yellow pages. I found a home at the Salvation Army's Bethesda Centre in London, Ontario. When I toured their facilities, I knew in my heart that it was the place for me. I couldn't put my finger on it, but something about the place felt warm. It felt like home. And I decided it would be. It was where I would live, be educated, get counseling, and receive prenatal care and parenting training. My mom and Bruce didn't blink at my decision. I guess they figured if I was old enough to make a baby, I was old enough to figure out what to do about it.

There was one more thing I needed to do—tell Jeremy. I hadn't spoken to him in weeks. I called him and told him we needed to talk in person. I have a feeling he knew why. It wasn't often I asked him for a face-to-face conversation. When we met, I was nervous, as one would expect. It was hard to look him in the eye. I hadn't a clue how he would react.

At first he didn't believe me. After I gave him a few days to let the news sink in, though, he finally came around enough to take my word for it. I was determined to clean up my lifestyle for this baby, but I didn't feel like Jeremy was ready. I had to face the fact that I was on my own.

I told him that I would be leaving for London. I made plans to start my new life at Bethesda by myself. I convinced myself that I didn't need anyone. And I was on a mission to prove how capable and responsible I could be.

seven

Emotions all twisted and hormones run wild
The weight of an adult, the fears of a child
Questions are racing, awaiting reply
Confusion sets in, I sit and I cry
I feel like I'm trapped in this nightmare I'm in
I feel like I'm losing, there's no way to win
My dreams have been broken, my plans rearranged
My attitude's different, my body has changed
I have to be careful of each move I make
And remember someone else's life is at stake
It's a lot to remember and a lot to go through
But somehow it's worth it to go on so blue
I'll find some more dreams and I'll make some new plans
'Cause I know I'll recover with my blood in my hands.

I was two months pregnant in the beginning of August 1993. Early on a summer morning, my mom and Bruce drove me to the Bethesda Centre, a large, nondescript brick building nestled in a quiet neighborhood off one of London's main city streets.

We pulled up to the front entrance. The tight knot in my belly unraveled. This was it. My new home. I felt anxious and uncertain.

> Having a baby when you're older and married is an exciting time in life. But when you're a teenager, you're facing a long, tough road. Trust me, there's nothing glamorous about it. If you can abstain from sex and prevent this huge life change, you're better off. If you already are a pregnant teen, however, do your best to be the best mom you can be.

After I unpacked from the car the few pieces of luggage I brought for my eight-month stay, my mom and I said our goodbyes. There were no tears. No quivering lips. I wouldn't even let my eyes water. I was calm, cool, and collected, pretending I was leaving for summer camp: *I'll be back before you know it, Mom. I won't forget to write and send pictures. I'll miss you. Bye.* But this certainly was no summer camp. I wouldn't return home having learned how to swim or ride a horse. I'd return with a baby.

I mastered a brave front while waving goodbye to my mom. When the car rolled down the small hill of a driveway and all I could see was fading taillights, the floodgates opened. Down tumbled tears of shame. Tears of remorse. Tears of fear. Tears for the unknown. As I gasped for air in the middle of a sob, I forced myself to calm down. All I wanted to do was check in and go to my room where I could be alone.

I picked up as many bags as I could carry and shuffled into the lobby. I looked around at the humbly furnished room. The linoleum floors shined and a few old paintings colored the drab walls. Through an open door in my immediate view, I could see a few teenage girls with rounded bellies sitting around a large square table making crafts. They were laughing, having fun. *I hope they like me.*

I was numb throughout the intake process. Most of it was a blur; I dealt the best way I knew how—get through the hard part with as little emotion as possible. A sweet staff member led me to my room, talking the entire way about how wonderful the center was, how terrific the rest of the girls were, how much fun everybody was having, and how she just knew I was going to love it here.

I nodded and smiled, letting her talk a mile a minute. It kept me from having to let out as much as a peep. I was afraid if I had the chance to talk, I wouldn't be able to hold myself together. And I didn't want to collapse like a house of cards in front of a stranger. She'd probably just feel sorry for me and blame my emotional outburst on hormones.

Once I settled in and got comfortable, Bethesda ended up being a haven for me. I found a home where I'd had none. An acceptance I couldn't find elsewhere. We were a hodgepodge of scared, young moms-to-be. Bethesda was home to all kinds of girls—girls with a wild streak, girls who always made the honor roll, girls from broken homes, girls from rich families, girls who used to party, and girls who were goody-two-shoes. Though we came from different backgrounds, we had two things in common: we were young, and we were pregnant.

I felt like I belonged. It was comforting to know I wasn't the only one treading unknown waters. Together we shared our loneliness and our pain and tried to encourage each other as much as possible.

There was plenty to do at the home. We didn't sit around all day watching TV and eating bonbons.

> If you are a teen mom or are pregnant, don't be discouraged by the tough reality you are facing. Yes, it's a challenge. But if you are determined, have emotional support, and are committed to being a good mother, you can do this. Take your journey one step at a time.

Half of each day we had to go to school, which included basic classes we would have taken in high school like math, science, and English. We also took parenting classes. We had individual counseling sessions. We had devotions. We cleaned and helped to maintain the facilities. We would even get a little creative and put on fashion shows, parading our big bellies around.

Every once in a while different speakers would visit and talk to us about the realities of motherhood. They helped shoot down any romantic fantasies we had about parenting. So many teenagers think having a baby is like having a doll. You spend all day dressing them up in cute clothes. You cuddle with them and take them places where people fawn all over them. And of course they never cry. While some of those ideas may be true to a certain extent, there was a whole lot more to having a baby than most of us at Bethesda realized.

> We are responsible for our actions and the decisions we make—no one else is. Instead of complaining about the consequences that come from making bad choices, we need to accept them and move forward.

There's nothing cute or exciting about sleepless nights. Constant crying. The cost of diapers, wipes, and formula. Postpartum depression. The end—at least for a while—of going to movies and parties with your friends. The loneliness. The end of "me" and the beginning of "we." Never mind having to do all of this on your own. In short, motherhood is a difficult journey. I'll never forget what one of the speakers told us: "Being a teen mom is no picnic. It's the hardest thing I've ever done in my life."

Something about what she said hit home. That day I determined that I had to be prepared for the worst. But no matter how hard it would be, I would be the best mom I could be and give my baby one hundred percent of me.

As much as Bethesda had going for it—and as good as it was for me—being there still wasn't always easy. I got homesick. And I wasn't always happy.

I didn't write much in my journal during this time. The few pages I scribbled focused on how miserable I was: "I'm so unhappy, but I play along to my friends and family. . . . I could sit in my room and cry for days, but I could also tear apart everything in this place. Crying's safer, it keeps me out of trouble. I'd sure like to let some of this anger out, though. God help me."

It wasn't until I was more than halfway through my pregnancy that I knew my spiritual life needed a major adjustment. I still had not forgiven myself for taking steps backward. I was stuck in shame. John and his wife, Sue, kept me from sinking any deeper.

John visited with me a few times at Bethesda. I especially looked forward to seeing him; he always made me feel a lot better, less homesick. John and Sue were like second parents to me (and still are today). I loved this adorable, hippie-looking couple. I remember spending the night with them at their home once while I was pregnant. They prayed with me and actually tucked me into bed. It was such a sweet and intimate gesture. I felt so loved, so cared for. With her thick brown mane and dark, piercing eyes, Sue was beautiful inside and out. She showered me with affection and always encouraged me. John always had some kind of fatherly advice to offer; I always felt I could talk to him about anything.

One afternoon when I must have been seven or eight months along, John called and announced that he was picking me up for church that evening. He didn't give me a choice in the matter. "You can't say no," he told me. "I'm already on my way."

On one hand, I didn't want to go. Church? I groaned. I hadn't been to church in months. I didn't want to listen to a sermon and feel more guilt.

On the other hand, I was happy to get out of the center for a while, and the church John wanted me to visit wasn't our home church. I figured I'd feel more comfortable in the company of strangers than with people I knew. So I went.

Somewhere between the singing and the sermon, I accepted responsibility for the poor choices I had made since I had first allowed God to run my life. After all, look where I ended up—partying and getting pregnant, becoming an unwed mom. If I truly believed God had a plan for my life, I wasn't going to get there by doing things my way. I knew I had to start living life God's way.

For a long time I had believed that God had rules just to have rules or as a means to control people. For instance, it was hard for me to wrap my mind around the "no sex before marriage" thing. If something felt right, how could it be wrong? Eventually I learned He has reasons for the guidelines He sets in place. They're not meant to keep us from having fun; they're created out of love, to protect and give us the best shot at being successful. God didn't want me to contract sexual diseases or get pregnant without marital support and stability for my baby or me. He knew the consequences that could come from doing some stupid things. Some of which, in my case, would be life changing.

I've also learned that a sexual relationship between teenagers (or adults, for that matter) can confuse the emotional state of the relationship. It becomes challenging to figure out if you're close because you're sexually involved or because you really have something special.

> It can be hard to forgive ourselves when we mess up. Once we realize and are truly sorry for our failures and the mistakes we have made, it's time to accept God's forgiveness and forgive ourselves.

That night at church I had to face God and I had to face myself. I knew I didn't deserve it, but I wanted another chance. I needed grace. I recommitted myself to God that night.

It took a lot for me to believe I could have a second chance, so praying for anything more was beyond the scope of my imagining. I didn't deserve anything else. But as I prayed, I thought about my baby. I begged God to at least, if nothing else, let him or her be healthy and have ten fingers and ten toes.

With that prayer, I journeyed into the final stages of pregnancy. Life wasn't a fairy tale after that. I still had a lot to learn. I had to mature spiritually and start work-

> God is a God of second chances. No matter what mistakes you've made or how far you've fallen, He will always give you another chance.

ing on some of my internal issues. One thing was certain—I wasn't ever going to go back to my former life. I knew God had a plan for my life. A good one. And I wasn't going to let it go.

The day I went into labor, I was a week overdue. My baby was pretty happy staying in the womb. He took his time and didn't rush his appearance. (Ironic, considering once he made his grand entrance, he would constantly be on the go. His speeds have always been fast and faster.)

So a week past my due date, I went to the hospital to be induced. It wasn't the magical moment I had imagined since I was a little girl. I had pictured this moment with my husband, the father of my baby, clutching my hand by my side. I would have given everything just to have Jeremy there—whether or not we were together—supporting me, cheering me on, and celebrating the arrival of the baby we had created. I did, however, have support from others: my mom; my friend Missy; Jeremy's mother, Kate; and his sister, Bonnie. They all stayed by my side in the hospital room until I was taken into the delivery room.

After the doctor broke my water, I immediately went into natural labor. I started dilating quickly, much to the doctor's surprise. Four hours later, I was ready to be wheeled into the delivery room. My mom came with me while Kate, Missy, and Bonnie waited anxiously in the waiting room.

After seven minutes of screaming and sweating, annoyed at the doctors and nurses who kept yelling at me to "push" (wasn't it obvious?), around one in the morning on Tuesday, March 1, 1994, at St. Joseph's Hospital in London, Ontario, Canada, I finally heard it . . .

The cutest little cry I have ever heard. Music to my ears. I kid you not, my precious baby boy sounded like he was singing.

The nurses wiped him off and laid him on my chest. My heart pounded. Was he healthy? Did he have ten fingers and ten toes? He was perfect. Seven pounds, fourteen ounces of squirmy, sweet perfection. I'd planned to call him Jesse, but when I saw my baby boy for the first time—when our eyes locked, the melodic crying faded to a whimper, and his tiny finger curled around mine—I realized he looked nothing like a Jesse.

"Hi, Justin," I whispered, wondering how on earth two messed-up teenagers could have created the most breathtaking baby in the entire universe. I was swept away by the most beautiful moment in my entire life, nestling my sweet baby against my skin. My mother beamed when she finally had the chance to hold Justin. She stared into his face, her eyes glowing with pride, with amazement, with gratitude. When it was Jeremy's mother's turn, she did much the same, gasping, "He looks exactly like Jeremy."

After all the visitors left and I found myself alone in the hospital with Justin, I finally had time to think. Something happens when babies are born. The world seems different, better. You care less about stupid things and you start thinking more about the future.

This was it. Justin and I were on our own. Something about his sweet, crinkly face and the adorable yawns where he resembled a baby lion hushed all the fears and questions that competed for my attention.

How are you going to take care of this precious baby on your own? One day at a time, I suppose.

Can you even afford a baby as a single mom?
I'll find a way.
What if he gets sick?
I guess we'll go to the doctor.
Where are you going to live?
I'll work out those details just like I worked out everything else.
What if? What if? What if?

Sure, the questions were still there, but I didn't have the time or energy to get bogged down by the weight of them. After all, I had a baby boy to care for.

eight

Justin's hungry
My house is a mess
I don't have time for all this stress
It's one in the morning
So tired
So blessed
I think I'll go get some rest

I stayed at Bethesda for a month after Justin was born. When I returned to the pregnancy home after the hospital, I was exhausted but elated. The girls were flipping out over Justin, oohing and aahing, taking turns holding him and asking me about every detail of the birth. I could tell that some of the girls who were expecting in a few short weeks looked more uneasy than others.

Eleven days after Justin was born, Jeremy saw our son for the first time. I was at my mom's house for a visit. At the time, he and I weren't together as a couple, but I wanted Jeremy to see his son. He wanted to see him too. As I sat at the kitchen table, cradling Justin in my arms and inhaling the scent of his newborn skin, I anxiously anticipated the knock on the door.

I wasn't sure how Jeremy was going to react. Would he be excited? Would he act like he didn't care? I wondered if the minute Jeremy saw the beautiful masterpiece we had created together, things would change. Maybe—and I hoped this wasn't just wishful thinking—we could even be a family. There had been so much brokenness in my life, I longed to have stability of my own.

> Many people falsely believe that having a baby will make a rocky relationship better. Unfortunately, it's not usually the case. Some women even believe that having a baby will make their boyfriend stay with them. Again, not true. Bringing a baby into an unhealthy relationship is a recipe for disaster. Don't put expectations on an innocent child to heal what has already been broken.

Don't get me wrong. I knew our relationship was toxic. But even in light of how unhealthy we were together, I was still hopeful. Maybe, just maybe, Justin was the missing link to making our relationship work.

When Jeremy walked through the door and first laid eyes on our son, he simply stared. He couldn't stop. I don't think a herd of elephants dancing in the room could have stolen Jeremy's attention away from Justin. Awe colored his face. He was mesmerized by our little baby. As Jeremy wrapped his strong arms around this tiny swaddled creature, his stare melted into Justin's sweet face. There's not much I remember from that day except for the image of a man locking eyes with his baby boy with the kind of love that can only come from a father's heart.

I stayed at my mother's house for a few weeks after I left Bethesda and before I moved into my own apartment. She became my shopping buddy as I prepared for my new life. We scoured garage sales, secondhand stores, and other charity organizations collecting things for my new apartment. I was making a home for Justin and me. I was excited to have my own stuff and didn't care that the furniture I bought was once or even twice used. I wasn't bothered by the worn fabric and tiny holes on the couches or that the kitchen table wobbled unless you stuffed rags underneath the legs. I appreciated everything I bought or received from generous and loving people and places like my church and Stratford House of Blessing, a local nonprofit organization.

I was on "mothers' allowance," the Canadian version of welfare, until I could support Justin and myself full-time. I didn't make much more than nine or ten thousand dollars a year, which included part-time jobs and social assistance. Justin and I didn't have much. It was a struggle to buy diapers and formula, but I managed to make it work. As poor as we were, my son never lacked for anything.

My mother and Bruce were amazing. They helped out financially whenever they could. They also took care of Justin when I needed a break. They often took Justin for a night over the weekend. When he got older, they helped pay for his hockey gear, membership fees, and so on. I'll always be grateful for their help. I realize a lot of single moms don't have that kind of support from their own parents.

For the first two years of Justin's life, he and I lived in an apartment complex a few minutes away from my mom and Bruce. Our first-floor, two-bedroom apartment was small but cozy. It was just the two of us,

> Raising a child is not about having a ton of money and giving him everything he wants. It's about loving him. Being committed to his well-being. Keeping him safe. Giving him the things that money can't buy.

so we didn't need much room. Outside of the questionable plumbing, the cheap aluminum window blinds that always bent, and the peeling paint on the walls, it was perfect. It was home.

After I moved into my own apartment, Jeremy started coming around a lot. Looking back, I was so naïve. Instead of making the mature choice not to get back together (for the hundredth time), I allowed the relationship to pick up where it had left off. Again. I followed the same pattern I had with Jeremy in the past. Getting back together seemed to follow right on the heels of each breakup. I basically shut my eyes to the truth that we weren't right for each other and hoped that everything would magically work out between us.

> We are often attracted to what is familiar, even though it may hurt. If all we know is abuse, being treated poorly, or constant drama, we are subconsciously drawn to those things. This is why we continually return to unhealthy relationships.

A few months down the road, I noticed a difference in Jeremy. He changed his life around and started focusing on our new family. We began spending every Sunday morning at church. We prayed regularly and even went to Bible study. I was amazed. This was a new and improved Jeremy. We even got engaged and set a wedding date.

For a short season, life was good. It seemed my little family was starting to take shape. As first-time parents, Jeremy and I enjoyed spending time together with our baby boy. Neither one of us could take our eyes off Justin. I melted at the slightest hint of a smile or a gurgling laugh. I loved how his tiny hands reached out for me, his mama. As I held Justin and pressed my nose against his sweet face, I disappeared into that distinct baby smell. He was a gift. He was entrusted to me. He was my life.

Despite how in love with Justin both Jeremy and I were, our relationship wasn't healthy enough to continue. We were still broken and needed to become whole on our own. I had a lot of healing and growing to do, and Jeremy needed to work on his own issues. The change he started to make didn't last long. Through a series of endless talks and a few heated fights I wish I could forget, we broke up for the last time. It was truly the end of us.

I've often wondered why I stayed in that relationship so long. Why was I so desperate for Jeremy and me to work out? I think it's simple—I was waiting for my fairy tale ending that included a lifetime of love and happiness, an adoring husband and, of course, the standard-issue white picket fence.

> No matter how much you try, you can't make another person fit in the place God should be. Nothing will satisfy like He does.

I was always waiting for the moment when I would be loved and accepted. And I thought Jeremy just might be the ticket to that fantasy. I hoped that things would change between us. That our toxicity would turn into something beautiful. That he would see the light and love me the way I longed to be loved. It was unfair of me to put so much expectation on Jeremy to meet all my unmet needs and fix all my brokenness. How could he? He was just as wounded as I was. And like me, he had no idea what a loving, nurturing relationship looked like.

It would take a long time, but eventually Jeremy and I got to the point where we maintained a healthy friendship. Though we've had our share of hurtful moments and on-and-off drama throughout the years, we've tried our best to keep our differences at bay. Today, I would consider Jeremy a friend.

> In order to love someone else in a healthy way, you have to learn how to love, value, and appreciate yourself first. If you struggle with self-hatred or low self-esteem and don't feel you deserve love, peace, and joy, how can you be part of a healthy, loving relationship?

If you know someone who is in a toxic relationship, don't judge them. Talk to them and find out why they choose to stay. Ultimately, you can't change people or their minds, but you can lend a listening ear, offer support, and be a good influence.

While Jeremy and I had our rough patches in the beginning of our son's life, we were eventually able to smooth them out for Justin's sake. We've never badmouthed each other in front of him or used him against each other to get our way. We made sure Justin knew that both of us loved and cared for him, even though we weren't together.

Contrary to what some media outlets may say, Jeremy didn't just show up when Justin became famous. Today, Jeremy is a totally different person than he was when we were younger. He has changed in many ways for the better. Being a father is his first priority. I'm proud of what a great dad he has become to Justin and his two younger children (from another relationship).

nine

It's not hard to be a single mom, but it is hard to be a good one. Single moms don't have it easy. It's lonely. Tiring. Nothing prepares you for being a mom, even if you have support. You can take a hundred parenting classes. You can listen to your mom, your friends, your neighbors, or your hair stylist talk about their experiences until your ears fall off. And you still won't be ready.

When you're on your own playing the roles of both parents, you're even less prepared. And when you're not even out of your teen years, you just got thrown into a whole different game. It's tough trying to swing the bat with that curve ball thrown at you. The pressure can at times feel overwhelming.

I felt like I had to do it all. I had to provide for Justin's physical, emotional, financial, and developmental needs. I didn't have a husband I could hand him off to if I needed an hour break. I had to suck it up and figure it out on my own. And as small as it may seem, not having a partner was also hard for me because I had to lug everything around myself. Do you know how strategic (and strong) you have to be to carry a baby, a diaper bag, and a bag of groceries while manipulating a stroller?

I survived single motherhood by sheer willpower and a ton of prayer. You do whatever you have to do. There really isn't much

> Any major life change (like becoming a mom as a teenager) requires accepting a new normal. Whether you're moving to a different state or going to a new school or your parent is getting remarried, you have to accept your new normal and make appropriate adjustments. During this tough time, talk to friends and family who love and will support and encourage you.

time to complain or wallow in self-pity when you're trying to change diapers, feed your baby, figure out why he's crying, find ways to come up with money for baby stuff on top of rent and utilities, and get educated to create a better future for you and your little one. Phew! There are so many responsibilities and worries you have to deal with—and usually with little sleep.

Like most single mothers, I quickly discovered the art of survival mode. I powered through and did what I needed to do to get through Justin's early years. If I was tired from being up all night and had to work all day, I'd drink an extra cup of coffee. If I came home from work after a stressful day and realized rent was due in a few days, I'd figure out a way to find the money. I came to accept that life isn't always fair. That good things don't always happen to good people. And that no one is immune to tough times. I had no time to live in a fairy tale, expecting Prince Charming to show up and rescue me. I had the precious responsibility of being a good mother to a baby who needed me.

When Justin was born, I hadn't finished high school. I knew I had to eventually go back and get my diploma. I wanted to; I just didn't have the money to pay someone to watch Justin while I was in school. My neighbor Mike would always remind me of the importance of education and encourage me to go back to school. He

If you are a teen mom and are struggling, here are some tips that will help:

- Take things one day—or even one step—at a time.
- Find a strong network of support (friends, family, your church, local organizations).
- Ask for help if you need it.
- Set a good example for your child. "Do as I say, not as I do" doesn't work.
- Take care of yourself physically, emotionally, and mentally.
- If you have an estranged relationship with your child's father, don't talk negatively about him in front of your child.
- Make sure your child is surrounded by positive role models. It takes a village to raise a child!
- And remember, the best thing you can give your child is love.

was a computer whiz. Mike came over one day to say hello. We chit-chatted for a few minutes while one-year-old Justin crawled around on the floor, babbling away and playing with Mike's shoelaces.

"So, Pattie . . ."

I knew what was coming.

"You gotta go back to school," he sweetly reminded me as he always did. "You need your diploma."

We had a long discussion that afternoon about my dilemma. While I complained, Mike listened and tried to be helpful. I didn't see him for a few weeks after we spoke.

You can imagine my surprise when I got a call from a local day care saying I needed to enroll Justin soon because someone had

Did you know that over 3 million teens drop out of high school every year?[14]

- 75 percent of dropouts commit crimes.[15]
- 90 percent of jobs are not available to dropouts.[16]
- Recent dropouts will earn $200,000 less than high school graduates, and over $800,000 less than college graduates, over their lifetimes.[17]
- Dropouts are about three times more likely to be on welfare than those who complete high school but do not attend college.[18]

dropped off a check paying for an entire year of day care. I almost dropped the phone. Who would do something like that? I knew my mom and Bruce couldn't afford it, and, well, I didn't know anybody who had the extra money to be so generous.

Somehow I found out it was Mike. When I thanked him, gushing my appreciation, he was bashful. His generosity was huge to me, but he didn't make too big of a deal out of it. There was only one thing he wanted in return: "One day, help someone else go to school." In other words, pay it forward.

Mike told me someone had helped him when he struggled financially in college. Instead of paying back the money, he promised to down the road help someone else finish school. I'll be forever grateful to him. His generosity is nothing short of a blessing, a miracle.

"It is more blessed to give than to receive."

(Acts 20:35)

I was surprised how much fun it was going back to school. I made a ton of friends quickly, which helped me to enjoy my classes and actually have a good time. My friends and I had a blast. I even still talk to some of them today.

I was nervous about going back to school at first, however. I didn't know what to expect. My life was totally different from

Education is important! Whether you are in school or have dropped out for whatever reason, make education a priority. It will help:

- Increase your IQ
- Equip you for college or the workforce
- Teach you to make better decisions
- Lay the foundation for a brighter future

I know your teenage years are supposed to be fun and carefree, but don't waste your precious years trying to fit in and be cool. Five years from now, it's not going to matter what you wore, what parties you were invited to, or how popular you were. However, it will matter what kind of education you received and what you're doing with it.

the last time I had walked the halls. I didn't sit in class stoned this time. My mind wasn't a million miles away while teachers droned on and on about math or literature. This time I showed up. I paid attention. I hung on every word the teachers spoke. And after school, I studied hard while little Justin slept.

I knew how important getting an education was if I wanted a better life for Justin and me. Nothing was going to stop me from focusing on my studies. I couldn't afford to take school lightly. It was my hope to get out of poverty, to build a future, to be an example for my son.

As a new mother, I had grown up. I was more mature than the other students. I worried about my future, about creating a stable life where I could give Justin the best possible chance of being successful. Most high school kids don't need to think about stuff like that. They have partying on the brain. They spend their time playing video games, picking out cool outfits, or just hanging out. They're more interested in Friday night football games than figuring out ways to pay the bills. And that's not a bad thing. Teens shouldn't have to worry about or be responsible for things far above their maturity level.

Though my life situation was nothing like that of the typical high school student and some of the kids knew I had a baby, no one knew how old I was. Because I looked young and was young at heart, it was assumed I was seventeen, just like everyone else. Except, of course, I wasn't. By then I was twenty. There were no extracurricular activities for me. No sports, dance recitals, or choir practices. As soon as the last bell of the day rang, I hurried to day care to pick up Justin.

That day care was such a gift. I appreciated that each day his teachers would write details about his day in a notebook. There aren't many earth-shattering things a one-year-old does in a matter of a few hours, but every now and then I'd read something that would make me smile . . . or shake my head.

For the most part, each day listed a different version of "Justin ate well" and "Justin took a great nap." Every now and then his teachers noted Justin doing unusual things, like biting. I was embarrassed to read "Justin is biting his friends again" or "Justin did better with biting and only bit one boy." Other than that, though, my son was a pretty happy-go-lucky kid.

When I recently reread that notebook, I was blown away at how many of Justin's personality traits and quirks back then are still the same today. The teachers always (and I mean always) made notes of how energetic he was, how he was always on the "go-go-go," and how he loved saying "hi" to everyone he passed (Justin was a ham and loved the attention). As anyone who knows him today will agree, he is still very energetic, busy, and friendly. Justin's love for music was also evident early on. His favorite time of the day was circle time, when the kids sang songs led by a teacher who played a keyboard. One entry especially cracked me up: "Justin's pants keep falling off, so we tied them with a string." Some things never change—I'm still telling Justin to pull up his pants. And he still doesn't listen.

I can't begin to count the number of nights those first couple of years when I'd lie awake in the wee hours of the morning, tossing and turning from worry. Most times Justin would be up not long after to eat, so there was no point trying to get comfortable. I'd stare at the red numbers on the alarm clock, my body exhausted but my mind racing. So many questions cluttered my mind.

Will I be able to finish high school?

How many diapers does Justin have left?

How will I pay for day care next year?

Will I ever go to college?

On and on my mind would spin with worry. So I prayed. A lot.

Don't think for a minute, though, that I looked at God as a vending machine, where I'd pop in a prayer and out would come a miracle. I do believe God will come through for us when we pray; I just didn't expect Him to instantaneously supply my needs while I sat back and watched TV all day or wasted the money I had on stupid things. From the day Justin was born, I was either in school, working, or looking for a job.

I prayed because I was in pretty desperate situations beyond my control. I prayed for basic things like rent money and food on

> *Worry never cured a thing. It doesn't do anything for you except make you tired, upset, and scared. "Can any one of you by worrying add a single hour to your life?" (Matthew 6:27).*

the table. Things that were hard for me to come up with on my limited income.

The answers to prayer always seemed to come at the last minute. Though I believed in miracles, having to wait for them wasn't fun. It was frustrating. And sometimes it even made me doubt God would take care of me.

> God is not a vending machine where you drop in a few coins and out pops whatever you want. Prayer is about connecting with Him on a deeper level. Talk to Him like you would talk to a friend.

But He did. In the craziest of ways. Random people at church, some of whom barely even knew me, would slip a check into my Bible when I wasn't looking. One time a group of ladies pulled up to my apartment and stocked my refrigerator and cupboards with groceries. Another time a man on a bus, a total stranger, walked up to me and said, "I really feel I am supposed to give this to you." He handed me an envelope full of cash, just enough money to cover my expenses that month.

Coincidence? Sheer luck? I don't believe that for a second.

John called one day and asked me for a favor. He had found a fourteen-year-old runaway named Liz on a park bench. She was homeless, cold, and hungry. He had talked to her for a while with one of his social worker friends. And though John wanted to help her out, he couldn't do much for her overnight and asked for my help.

My heart jumped. Of course she could spend the night. Just imagining this young, helpless girl sleeping outside in an unfamiliar city broke my heart. God only knew what dangers lurked around and what kind of trouble she could get into. I told John to bring her right over.

I was surprised when Liz first walked through the door that night. She looked much younger than fourteen. Her strawberry blonde hair was pulled to the side in two neat ponytails, and freckles dotted her face. She didn't look directly in my eyes when she spoke a breathy "Hey." I knew she felt uncomfortable. I was a stranger, a stranger she had no reason to trust.

John was right, however. We instantly bonded. She was one of the sweetest, brightest girls I had ever met. The next morning I asked John if I could keep her. I was serious. Liz had nowhere to go. At the least I could give her a place to stay.

I wasn't sure how this would all work out; I just figured it would. John thought my offer was sweet but didn't think it was possible. Who would allow a twenty-year-old single mother to take in a fourteen-year-old runaway? It was a ridiculous thought.

John and I found out Liz had been in and out of so many foster homes that her social worker was at her wit's end. She ran away from every foster home and wouldn't stay in any one for longer than a month. The social worker was desperate to find a home for Liz where she'd stay put. At that point, I don't think they cared where she stayed. So one day I got a call from the social worker. "Here's the deal, Pattie. If Liz agrees to stay with you, we'll interview you, check out your apartment, and then make a decision."

> Don't be afraid to take a risk and help others. Even a small gesture of compassion will brighten someone's day. Share a smile. Talk to someone who is feeling lonely. Sit with a new student at lunch. Help carry an elderly neighbor's groceries from her car to her house.

When Liz moved in, it quickly became obvious our two-bedroom apartment was too small. The three of us were always bumping into each other. Liz moving in meant it was time to move out. But how? Where? And, oh yeah, there was that little problem of money.

I barely had anything left after using my welfare checks to pay for rent, utilities, and food. But I wasn't too worried. I prayed. And I gave my notice to the landlord.

I had two months to find a place I could afford. More than enough time, or so I thought. With my measly budget, it wasn't the easiest house hunt. I searched in the paper, asked around, and browsed online. I prayed and I waited. Nothing.

> It's hard to have a positive attitude all the time, but being optimistic no matter how bad things look will help you get through the tough times. Keep the faith. Keep believing. Trust that things will work out and more than likely, they will.

At the end of every church service, I asked my friend Tim for prayer about my apartment search. We did the same thing each week: I'd ask for prayer and he'd pray. Sunday after Sunday, I prayed the same prayer with no answer in sight. Three weeks before I was supposed to move out, I was getting pretty uneasy. I prayed louder, stronger. Still nothing. A week later, I had a full-blown panic attack. Where would we live? It wasn't just me I was responsible for. I had to provide for a baby boy and a teenage girl!

Though he had watched my prayer go unanswered week after week, Tim didn't seem a bit discouraged. He tried to calm me down. "I really believe God is going to teach you a lesson in faith through all this," he said.

I rolled my eyes at that. *Are you kidding me?* I looked at him, nowhere near convinced, and said, "If I'd just found an apartment, I could see how that could be true. But at this point, I'll be on the streets. This situation isn't giving me faith, it's making me doubt."

He smiled. "Sometimes God makes you wait, Pattie. And then wait some more. And sometimes even right at the last minute, He makes you wait just a little bit longer *and then* He comes through.

It's how you learn to trust Him. When God makes things happen, you can't take the credit."

Another week passed. Nothing. I was beyond frustrated. Was this some sort of sick joke? Were we supposed to live out on the streets? Was that really what God wanted?

On the Wednesday before the three of us would be homeless, my mom called. She sounded excited. "There's a new listing in the paper for an apartment on Elizabeth Street, and it's available immediately."

Hope.

Finally.

I drove with Liz and Justin across town to talk to the landlord. The three of us must have been quite a sight: a teenager dressed in funky clothes, a tired-looking mom who looked like a teenager herself, and a rambunctious two-year-old toddler. Oh well. We put on our biggest smiles and prayed the landlord would miraculously believe we were the perfect tenants for the place.

The apartment was beautiful, complete with three bedrooms, a loft, an outside patio, and even a fireplace. The rent was cheap and included all the utilities. It seemed too good to be true. *It's gotta be a dream*, I thought as I walked carefully on the dark hardwood floors and grazed my fingers on the fresh coat of paint that adorned the walls.

After he finished showing us the lovely backyard where I knew Justin would love playing, the landlord spoke. "Listen. I could rent this apartment out to anyone. I've showed it to a lot of people, and I even have more appointments after you." He paused for a few seconds, carefully choosing his next words. "But I've been praying about who to rent this apartment to, and I believe I'm supposed to rent it to you."

It sounds crazy, right? I know it does. But I promise you, it's true. I realized that Tim was spot-on. The whole experience really did increase my faith. We lived in that beautiful apartment for

> If you look at your life, no matter how young you are, I'm sure you'll see times when you've experienced unexpected help, kindness, and generosity from others. The best repayment is to pay it forward. Show someone else the same kind of goodness that was shown to you.

almost three years. We were never late on our rent once, although we eventually got kicked out because it seemed Justin made too much noise. Between the drum playing, loud music, and typical toddler banging, we were a little too noisy for our neighbors.

Liz stayed with us for a year and a half total. She was probably more of a gift to me than I was to her (though years later she wrote me a beautiful poem about how she was convinced I showed her the true meaning of love). Liz helped around the house and with Justin, who adored her. I like to think Justin and I were positive influences, because after moving in she stopped stealing and using drugs. She also enrolled in school full-time and started going to church.

I was glad to have been given the opportunity to let her stay with us. I've been on the receiving end of so many blessings by random strangers, it was the least I could do to pay it forward.

A JOURNEY
through the YEARS

My mom with my dad

My mom, my dad,
Chris, and Sally

Early years . . .

Still stealing kisses today

Mom and Bruce on their wedding day

Our new family:
Chuck, Candie,
Chris, Mom, me,
and Bruce

Full of smiles at five and six

Posing
with Bruce

At my sixth
birthday party

The house
I grew up in

Dressed up
for church with
my friend Robbie

With friends
on my ninth
birthday

Ready to perform
at the Stratford
Festival
at age ten

Growing up—love that '80s hair!

Expecting Justin

Walking the "runway"
at a Bethesda fashion
show

My mom with me
and a newborn
Justin

Bonnie and
Grandma Kate
with Justin at
the hospital

Father and son

With Grandpa George
and Grandma Kathy

With Grandma Kate

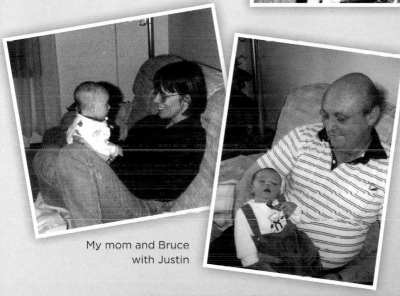

My mom and Bruce
with Justin

Four generations—
my mom,
my grandma,
Justin, and me

Me and baby Justin

My beautiful baby boy

First birthday

At the lake

Hanging out with his dad

A ham from the start

Snuggling with my boy

First day of public school

Justin's first love: sports

Fun times camping

Being goofy

Our first trip to Atlanta

In the cockpit

Scooter and Justin
clicked from the start

GROWING UP *so fast . . .*

but forever my
SWEET BOY

ten

Growing up, my son was a combination of Curious George, Dennis the Menace, and Bart Simpson rolled into one. Women I knew who had multiple children actually told me that just watching Justin wore them out. The kid couldn't sit still to save his life. I'm not even joking when I say that Justin actually bounced off walls. Full of life, he was born ready to brave the world with a mischievous grin and a whole lot of energy.

As a baby, Justin wasn't much of a cuddler. As soon as he was able to roll and tumble about, he wanted out of my arms so he could explore on his own. He was always seeking independence. He'd loosely hold on to my hand while reaching out with the other to see what exciting new adventures existed beyond my reach, even if it was only a few steps away. Sometimes this curiosity got him into trouble.

"Boy, n.: a noise with dirt on it."

—Not Your Average Dictionary

The few times I could afford to buy some new clothes, Justin and I took trips to the mall. I'd browse through the clothing racks and play peekaboo with him. Pretending I didn't know where he was, I'd call his name while he hid and giggled loudly inside the clothing rack I rummaged through. After a minute or two, I'd dramatically push aside a section of clothes, find him laughing hysterically inside of the rack, and yell "Peekaboo!" to his squealing delight. (How I miss those days!)

While I looked for a winter jacket on one such trip, two-year-old Justin and I were playing our tenth round of peekaboo. This time, however, when I pushed aside the coats and yelled "Peekaboo," Justin was nowhere to be found. I panicked. I threw down the jackets I'd draped over my arm and dashed around the store, madly searching inside each clothing rack to find my little guy. He wasn't anywhere. Not in the rack of shirts. Not in the clearance rack. Justin was nowhere in the store.

My heart pounded and my palms were thick with sweat. I hadn't been browsing for more than two minutes during our game; I didn't understand how he could disappear so fast. *Help! Where is my son?* I immediately called out to the store clerk, who helped me look for him. Maybe Justin somehow found his way to the back of the store? Five minutes passed and still no sign of him.

I ran out into the mall, calling Justin's name and asking passersby if they had seen a two-year-old blond-haired little boy wearing a red shirt and blue jeans. They hadn't, but they were kind enough to help me look for him. A security guard had run over to help me by that time and had radioed all the mall employees to keep an eye out for a missing two-year-old boy. Ten minutes had passed and Justin was still missing. It's a mother's worst nightmare. I was in hysterics, walking in and out of every store calling out "Justin! Justin! Justin!" I desperately hoped that at any minute he would turn the corner and run into my arms. But there was no sign of my son.

Finally, the security guard heard a buzz on his walkie-talkie. Someone had spotted Justin at the other side of the mall in the children's play area. I'd never run so fast in my life. I was panting and out of breath by the time I reached Justin. My lungs were about to explode. "Justin," I called out. My frantic heart was finally able to calm down at the sight of him safe and sound. My son, of course, hadn't the faintest clue I had spent the last ten minutes in an absolute frenzy trying to find him. "Look, Mom," he squealed when he saw me, without the slightest care in the world. He pointed to the rocket ship kiddie ride he was trying to climb. "A wocket sip!"

Feeling equally relieved and irritated, I grabbed him. I hugged him so hard and so close, he tried to squirm his way out of my tight grip. "Don't you ever do that again," I said sternly, wiping away the wisps of blond hair that were always covering part of his eyes. My voice softened. "Honey, don't you ever, ever, ever leave Mommy

> Disciplining a child isn't easy, but it's important. I knew I had to be consistent with Justin and not let him get away with stuff. But boy, it was tough, because he was so darn cute! I could never stay mad at him for too long.

again." Finally able to wriggle free from my bear hug, he grinned from ear to ear and nodded his head. "Okay, Mommy! Can I pay on the wide now?"

Justin had a knack for pushing boundaries. He didn't like the word *no* very much. He loved to test me to see if I really meant it when I said it.

For instance, Justin knew the VCR (no DVDs back then) was off-limits. He'd walk over to the table where it lay, put his hand a few inches above the VCR, and look straight at me. "No, Justin," I'd warn. "You can't touch that." He'd quickly yank back his hand, his eyes still fixed on mine.

Not but a few seconds later, he'd slowly reach his hand out again near the VCR. I'd repeat the warning. "No, Justin." Without blinking, he'd yank back his hand again. When he'd reach his hand toward the VCR for the third time as I said, "No, Justin," in an I-mean-business tone, he would pause for a second, look at me, then quickly reach out and pound crazily on the VCR with his hand. Then he'd run toward the other side of the room, as far away from me as possible. He knew he was in deep trouble.

By the time he was two years old, he'd already seen more than his share of time-outs. When I'd make him sit in a corner for whatever trouble he got into, sometimes Justin would turn around to face me, pouting his cherry lips and innocently blinking his big puppy dog eyes. He'd shrug his shoulders and raise his hands with his palms out. With toddler frustration, he'd whine, "Awww, come on, Mom! But I'm ohneee two!"

> I loved homeschooling Justin and being his one and only teacher. If I could have afforded it, I would have done it his entire school career.

He was so cute, it was hard not to bust out laughing. "If you're old enough to know that, Justin, you're old enough to go in the corner," I'd say, doing my best not to smile.

When Justin was around three, I started homeschooling him, which I continued up until he was in first grade. It was an honor to be the one to give him the foundation for his future education. I taught him how to read and write. Justin was a learning machine. By the time he was four, he was reading full sentences on his own.

As a part of the curriculum, I taught him about the Bible and helped him put verses to memory. Friends and family would be amazed at how quickly Justin learned and especially how he could recite a Bible verse verbatim when prompted by a chapter and verse reference. My son blew me away. He knew by heart at least fifty verses at one time and could recite them without missing a beat. It was impressive.

I enrolled Justin in public school because I had to work; we needed the money. Though I started him a year early and he had already completed the first-grade curriculum at home, I wanted to enroll him in a French school, so I let him repeat the year with kids his own age. While he was in school, I worked part-time at Zellers, a Canadian version of Walmart.

Justin got kicked out of his class the first day for making fart noises with his armpits. His teacher didn't have much patience and couldn't handle Justin. She immediately put him into a different first-grade class. She was the first of many teachers who would get fed up with my son. Justin wasn't purposely rebellious. His mischief was playful, even charming. He sometimes got in trouble for things he didn't even realize were wrong. Like the time he was suspended from Catholic school.

Justin loved movies and would often repeat lines from them. When he was around seven years old, he watched a movie called *Good Burger.* In one scene, a customer at a burger joint is complaining to Ed, a guy who works at the restaurant, about the hamburger he ordered. After he is done yelling, the angry customer storms out of the place and yells over his shoulder to Ed, "See you in hell!" Ed doesn't get that it's an insult and responds kindly, "Okay, see you there!" The scene was cute and funny, meant to make you laugh.

One afternoon when Justin rode the bus home from school, the Catholic bus driver wished him a good day as she let him off. Justin smiled, waved, and told her, "See you in hell, Bev!" He was suspended the next day. Justin wasn't trying to be mean, just funny. Unfortunately, the bus driver didn't appreciate my son's humor. He was always getting into trouble and pushing boundaries. It almost seemed like Justin would get suspended at least once a year for silly things like throwing snowballs or playing with bang snaps (the mini firecrackers you throw on the ground that make a popping sound).

Strong-willed children are leaders by nature.

A bright kid, Justin got bored easily. As he got older, I noticed his teachers either loved him or couldn't tolerate him. Some called him a leader. Others didn't know how to handle him and became frustrated. All the kids in his class, however, liked and wanted to be around

I often talk to parents of children with ADD or ADHD who get into a lot of trouble. While Justin wasn't formally diagnosed with either, the signs were obvious. Justin was always distracted, he was creative, he was always doing several things at one time, and he couldn't sit still. I've learned that these unusually strong-willed kids are most often too smart for their own good. They're leaders in the making and need to be encouraged and shown how to redirect their energy in a positive way. Many great leaders of yesterday and today had attention difficulties; some were even known for being troublemakers as children.

Justin. I remember one teacher used to say that she had thirty kids and Justin. If Justin was happy and behaving, the other kids followed suit. If he was being a troublemaker, the other kids copied his behavior.

I noticed Justin's musical talent very early on. It was hard not to; the boy had amazing rhythm. Even before he turned a year old, he could clap on beat to any song. When he was one, I'd bang out some beats and Justin would imitate me bang for bang as he sat in the high chair. He was a natural. He'd play the "drums" anywhere he found a flat surface: on pots and pans, chairs, countertops, the kitchen table, the bathroom sink—nothing was off-limits.

Justin got his musical abilities from both Jeremy and me. I had grown up singing and dancing, and Jeremy's side of the family was also gifted. Kate, Jeremy's mom, was a very talented singer/songwriter, and others on her side of the family were also musically gifted. Grandma Kate regularly sent us money for drum lessons when Justin was young. Jeremy too was involved with Justin's music. He always encouraged Justin and would also teach him songs on the piano.

So music was always a part of our lives. I had a lot of talented friends who would often come over for jam sessions. I loved to write and sing. My friend Jesse and I had many writing sessions at all hours. We actually sang at a couple of open mic sessions at a local hangout. One time we even had someone approach us and ask if we were looking for a manager. We laughed hysterically. Yeah, right! We were just playing music for fun. We did, however, use Jesse's multitrack recorder (nothing as cool as GarageBand) to make home recordings of our songs (which I can't seem to find anywhere!).

At home, I'd sing and play on my keyboard, the used Yamaha I bought for $400 when I was ten. I purchased it using money I earned from acting in the Stratford Shakespeare Festival.

When Justin was two years old, I bought him a mini drum kit. Without any lessons or directions, he picked up the sticks and started pounding away. He played for an hour. My friends and I watched in amazement as this pint-sized kid with tousled hair and half of his lunch coloring his T-shirt kept a perfect steady beat. With his signature grin plastered on his face, Justin bopped his head up and down, keeping in time with the rhythm. He loved playing the drums so much, when he was four I got him a djembe, a goatskin-covered African drum that had a different type of sound.

By this time, Justin was playing complicated beats and could easily keep up during a jam session with my friends. He was so good at the drums that I took him for lessons. I'll never forget the first time I brought Justin to the music studio. We walked through the glass door into the classroom. A shiny drum set sat in one corner. The teacher, Lee Weber, had his back toward us as he shuffled paperwork on a desk in the opposite corner.

"Hi, Mr. Weber," I said. "Justin Bieber's here for his first lesson."

With his back still turned toward us, the teacher let us know he'd be with us in a minute. I hoped the minute wouldn't be longer than five. Justin wasn't so great at sitting still and waiting.

Before we even had a chance to sit down, Justin made a beeline toward the drum set. "Justin!" I shouted, just as he hopped on the stool and grabbed a pair of drumsticks. Mr. Weber, still buried in paperwork, heard the commotion. Without looking up he assured us, "It's fine, Justin can play." I bet he was expecting to hear some little four-year-old kid bang away on the thing like a toy.

Justin started doing his thing. As he pounded out complex rhythms, he caught the attention of other students nearby. They gathered around the open door, trying to get a peek at who was playing. When Justin banged his last beat, the teacher had already dropped whatever he was doing and was standing next to me. His mouth stretched to the floor in shock. The kids outside the door went wild. One of them squeaked to Mr. Weber, "That kid is amazing! If you're his drum teacher, I want you to give me lessons!"

Mr. Weber couldn't contain his awe. "This is his first day. I haven't even given him a lesson yet. That's all him!"

After a few lessons from his first teacher, Justin went on to take lessons on and off for about six years from well-known local musicians including Wayne Brown and Mike Woods and a teacher we called "DLG." He got his first real drum kit when he was around nine.

Justin was a visual learner. He'd watch someone play something and be able to instantly copy what they did, whether they strummed the guitar or pounded out chords on a keyboard. And he played by ear. He could listen to a song and be able to play the exact melody and harmony and beat note for note. Every Sunday at church during worship, Justin sat on the steps of the stage mesmerized by each band member. His eyes bounced from keyboard to drums to guitar, mentally recording the details of each instrument and player as they played.

Justin especially loved to experiment with different instruments. When my friends were over, Justin had a ball. Most times he kept the beat for us by playing his mini drum kit or the djembe. I always kept instruments around the apartment, some given to us by friends and some I bought for cheap at yard sales. Justin would fiddle around with them whenever he wanted. He was amazing

We are all born with natural gifts, talents, and abilities. It's important to recognize them and nurture them. If you are not sure what you're good at, ask yourself:

- What am I passionate about?
- What do I enjoy doing?
- What skills or talents come naturally to me?

Whether it's playing the piano, writing poems, playing soccer, building things, painting, or even encouraging others—take the time to explore those things. Take classes or lessons. Do research on what others are doing in those same areas. Don't let your passions sit idle. Do something with them.

at almost everything he tried. Justin even started writing songs as early as six years old.

Music was an outlet, a creative way for us to have fun and keep busy. While I encouraged Justin's natural talent, I never forced him into anything. I was proud of his talents and abilities, but I was careful not to pressure him to learn music. I always let him decide what he wanted to learn. If he wanted to play an instrument, I got him one. If he asked for lessons, I'd find the money to make it happen.

As good as he was at music, though, it wasn't his first love. There was one thing Justin loved more: sports. While music was a fun hobby, sports were his life. My little boy excelled at every sport he played. He practically skated before he learned how to walk. From the time he was five years old, he was on the all-star travel team for soccer and hockey each year. After he started playing sports,

I think so often we expect our parents to give us the coolest gadgets, buy us the coolest clothes, and take us cool places. But the best investment they can give us is their time. Sadly, some kids have parents who have never attended their football games or dance recitals.

Don't blow off your mom and dad if they want to spend time with you and are interested in what you do. That's one way they are showing their love.

anytime I asked Justin what he wanted to be when he grew up, his answer was always the same: "A professional hockey or soccer player."

My son was not just good at sports and music, though; he could do so many different things well. Justin could skateboard, solve a Rubik's Cube in under two minutes, and even juggle. He won regional chess championships and junior golf tournaments. I know, I know, I sound like such a proud mama—and I am—but I was fascinated by all Justin's talents. He was competitive, bright, and coordinated. The kid could do it all.

Investing my time in Justin's life was important, especially since I was a single parent. I had plenty of opportunities to work in a factory during the afternoons and evenings, but I never entertained the idea. I held down a few random part-time jobs when Justin was in school so I could be home by the time he got there. Sure, I could have made more money had I worked the odd hours when Justin wasn't in school, but it wasn't worth it. I wouldn't sacrifice my time with him for a bigger paycheck. Besides, I loved hanging out with him. He was my little buddy.

Faith was a big deal in our home. We went to church on Sundays and Bible study or youth group once a week. I even taught him in Sunday school. I prayed with Justin every night. We had a bedtime routine where I would tuck him in "as snug as a bug in a rug" and we'd pray together and talk about everything. There were times this fifteen-minute bonding session turned into hours. It was our quality time together. Our way of connecting. And we shared most of our laughs during this time. The nights we stretched our routine out, we would be so tired and would giggle about the stupidest things. I cherish those memories. And Justin and I still talk about them to this day.

Stratford has been named the prettiest city in the world because of its many beautiful parks. Justin and I practically lived in Queens Park during the spring and summer months. We took long walks along the Avon River, admiring the old Victorian mansions that line the waterway.

We chased each other up and down the stone pathways flanked by weeping willow trees and raced over picturesque footbridges. We fed the stunning white swans that dotted the lake. I watched Justin Rollerblade for the first time on the walking trails around the manicured gardens. When we were hungry, I set up picnic lunches on the tiny island just over one of the footbridges. Justin always begged me to go on the paddleboats, but I couldn't afford it. I felt terrible I never had the extra money to give my boy a ride.

Two of the town's theaters were right in the park area, so when it was time for the annual Shakespeare Festival, Justin and I joined the massive crowds and people-watched. Because I had performed in this festival as a child, spending time there with Justin had a special place in my heart. It brought back memories. Good memories. Memories of when I dressed up in elaborate costumes and acted my heart out in front of thousands of people. Memories of me as a happy child in a happy place.

As a single mom, though I was in a different season of my life than I had thought I'd be, it was priceless to be able to enjoy time with my son, nurturing him and watching him grow. As hard as it was raising him as a single mom, every moment was worth it.

eleven

W hen Justin was around six and we moved to what would be our last apartment in Stratford, I needed to find a more permanent job to help support us. I asked my friend Mike (the guy who had paid for Justin's day care) for advice. Because I was pretty good at computers and was creative, he thought I should look into website design.

I took Mike's advice, and in 2002 I graduated from Conestoga College with a degree in website design and joined a local technology company called Blackcreek. Outside of doing web design and manning the front desk when necessary, I also subbed for the instructors in the computer classes they offered. If the company needed someone to teach basic computer courses like "Intro to Email" or basic Microsoft programs, I pitched in. I traveled to different schools, senior centers, and even people's homes for one-on-one lessons.

A couple of years later when Blackcreek restructured, I was let go, but my boss wanted to help me somehow. He knew I wanted to start my own business doing website design, so he gave me a computer to help me on my way. Whenever Blackcreek found themselves overworked and understaffed, they would also pass on their clients to me. I was grateful for the support.

> It's empowering when others believe in you. Sometimes people even believe in you more than you do. But some of us aren't so lucky.
>
> If you don't have the support or encouragement of others to help you follow your dreams or decide the next steps for your life, at least believe in yourself.

Though I worked full-time, I spent a lot of time with Justin when he came home from school. If I wasn't with him at soccer or hockey practices or games, we'd hang out on the ugly, old, yellow shag carpet in the living room and play board games or music.

We loved being spontaneous and taking road trips to nowhere. It was our special bond. We'd hop in my $700 early 1980s Oldsmobile Cutlass Supreme, a boat of a car, and take off on random adventures. Driving down long stretches of highway with the windows down, we'd blast the radio, constantly fighting about what station we should listen to. I'd set the dial to a country station and Justin would groan and switch it back to a pop one. We'd playfully battle it out between the likes of Faith Hill and Nelly.

There was one type of music we both agreed on—R&B. When I was pregnant and while Justin grew up, I listened to Boyz II Men all the time. Justin became a huge fan of the band. He listened to Boyz II Men on repeat, memorizing every word and mimicking all the melodies. Today Justin says this band inspired him and taught him how to sing.

We often took trips to visit my friends in Toronto, an hour and a half away. We loved walking around downtown and listening to the street musicians. On each trip we took, my friend Nathan came with us. We didn't know the streets of Toronto very well, so having him around always made me feel safe.

I remember our first trip, when Justin was six. He took his djembe with him, ready to jam with one of my friends later that day. As we walked around the city, I couldn't stop staring at Justin. He was mesmerized by the sights and sounds of the city—the noisy mesh of car horns and buses, the hustle and bustle of people scurrying by, the soaring skyscrapers.

He even got his first taste of playing in front of a crowd. We stopped to listen to a street musician. Justin sat down next to him for a few minutes and pounded away in perfect time on his djembe. He wasn't there long. But that little taste of playing in public was enough to make Justin want to come back to the city just to play music on the streets.

Sure enough, not long after that first trip, Justin asked if we could take a trip to Toronto to play. Of course we could. We drove down to the city, continuing our never-ending tug-of-war about what we would listen to. As we walked around downtown, we noticed the *Speaker's Corner* booth in our coming path. For only a few dollars, you could get a few minutes of recording time to rant, rave, sing, dance, or do pretty much whatever you wanted to do. The most entertaining videos were aired on the *Speaker's Corner* television show.

I had an idea. I asked Justin if he wanted to sing a song and play his djembe on camera for TV. "Yes!" he answered enthusiastically. As soon as the camera rolled, Justin started pounding away on the drum. He stared directly into the camera and sang along to the beats he banged out. "My name is Justin." *Ba dump bump bump.* "I'm six years old." *Ba dump bump bump.* Two minutes passed and people started gathering around on the sidewalk. They elbowed each other and whispered how amazing this little boy was. Justin barely noticed the attention; he was so focused.

After the camera stopped recording, Justin walked out of the booth and continued his mini concert in front of a growing audience. Having watched street musicians, he knew what to do. He whipped off his baseball cap and threw it on the ground in front of him, continuing to sing and play.

I have to be honest: though he was entertaining and fun to watch, a part of me wasn't sure how to feel. Though a ton of musicians busked on the streets of downtown Toronto, some people took it as a form of begging. But I shrugged it off. I didn't care what people thought. Watching Justin made me smile. I simply enjoyed his first time busking, the first of many to come.

Justin wanted to busk all the time. While we couldn't take weekly trips to Toronto because I didn't have the extra gas money or the time, we spent many afternoons and nights in downtown Stratford. We loved going downtown. It's such a pretty place full of historic buildings, cute boutiques, and artsy coffee shops.

The Avon Theatre, Justin's favorite busking spot, is nestled right in the heart of downtown and was always packed on weekends and weeknights. Justin would sit on the theater steps strumming on a guitar that looked too big for him and singing his heart out. Like clockwork, crowds would quickly gather and start piling money, dollar bills and change, into the empty guitar case at his feet.

Because Justin was young (and extremely talented, of course), the crowd tended to be more generous with him than with the older buskers. People would toss ten- and even twenty-dollar bills Justin's way. He probably made thousands of dollars playing music on the streets. In one summer alone, he made enough money to buy us a vacation to Disney World. We had never before been on vacation, so when Justin asked me if he could take us there with the money, of course I said yes!

I loved watching Justin perform. For about two hours, he'd sing all sorts of songs—worship songs, pop songs, and ones he made up days earlier or even on the spot. He was so confident, bellowing out tunes as if he'd been performing his whole life. It was fascinating watching a crowd of people mesmerized by my little boy. I was so proud.

Justin begged me to take more trips to Toronto, where he clutched his djembe and guitar as we roamed the streets. Justin was in his glory when he performed in front of random strangers. He had a playful energy that attracted people, young and old. Street musicians in their twenties would shake their heads at this miniature musical genius. They'd pass by with their tattered clothes and greasy hair and throw a few bills his way.

One of my favorite memories is of one particular trip to Toronto when Justin was nine years old. We were walking around downtown, with our faithful escort Nathan, when something on a street corner caught Justin's eye. There on the sidewalk were two beat-up drum sets. A pail sat in the middle of the two instruments with two pairs of drumsticks sticking out the top. A sign leaning against one of the bass drums exclaimed in bold black letters, "Pay $2 and play the drums with us!" Two twentysomething musicians were chatting with a passerby who had just thrown two bucks into the pail. When he started jamming with one of the musicians, Justin's eyes opened even wider. I knew what was coming.

> I'll never forget those street musicians who gave Justin their last dollar and in return made him promise to keep on playing his music and never give up.

When the jam session was over, Justin tugged at my arm. "Mom, can I play with them? Please? I'll even use my own money." How could I say no?

Justin practically threw down the guitar and djembe he had been carrying. He dumped two dollars in the bucket and picked up a pair of drumsticks. One of the musicians came over to him and tousled his hair. "How ya doin', little buddy?" I'm sure that just like Justin's first drum teacher, Lee Weber, he was expecting Justin to bang on the thing without rhyme or reason. The other musician stood a few feet away. Leaning against a lamppost, he smiled and waved to us.

Justin and the first guy hopped on their stools. Justin was ready to go, drumsticks in hand, his feet tapping the concrete in anticipation.

"You ready, buddy?" the drummer called out. "Here we go. A one, a two, a one two three."

The guy started playing a rhythm. My son joined in on the offbeat, playing his little heart out. Justin sounded amazing. He was just doing what he did so well and loved to do.

The drummer couldn't believe his ears. He shook his head in disbelief and whistled, "Holy smokes!" Realizing how good Justin was, the drummer started following his lead. The two of them jammed away, banging out contagious rhythms that you couldn't help but tap your feet to.

The other musician who had been taking a break started grooving. "Yeah, man," he yelled and slapped his thighs to the beat. Then he grabbed the empty pail and whipped a pair of drumsticks out of his back jeans pocket. Kneeling down on the pavement, he started banging on the plastic pail, adding a unique sound to the drums.

The three of them were amazing. Sticks were flying so fast they looked invisible. The passionate beats were flawless. I looked at Justin and smiled. He was having the time of his life.

The sidewalk started getting really crowded as passersby gathered around the musical spectacle. I stood shoulder to shoulder with people, barely able to move. Heads bobbed up and down in time with the music.

Just when I thought this performance couldn't get any better, the guy pounding on the pail suddenly jumped up on a streetlight. He started banging away at the top with his drumsticks. *Tink-tat-tink-tink-tat-tink-tink-tink.* Justin stared at the lonely pail on the sidewalk, and in the middle of playing, he jumped off the drum set and started playing on the pail. What a treat. He had never before played the pail, but he had no trouble following along and creating his own beats.

As the crowd cheered, a group of teenagers cleared a circle in the middle of the mob. They started breakdancing, spinning on their heads and doing flips. As Justin played the bucket, he couldn't stop staring at the dancers. Little Justin dropped the drumsticks on the sidewalk and made his way to the dancer's circle. He whipped off his sweater as he walked, and the crowd cried out, "Ooooh!" *Oh no you didn't!*

Justin busted out some moves that he had just learned from my friend Nathan. A natural performer, he egged on the young people who surrounded him by throwing his hands in the air, asking them if they wanted more. The crowd whooped and whistled.

After a few minutes, I could tell Justin was done. His attention span was running out. Sure enough, Justin looked at me and nodded his head. I knew it was time to go. By that time, there was so much activity going on between the drumming, the beats, and the dancing, it was easy for us to slip away almost unnoticed.

Justin's eyes were glowing. I could practically hear his heartbeat pounding wildly through his soaked T-shirt. "Mom, that was amazing!" he exclaimed, his face flushed.

As we started walking away from the crowd, two older, raggedy-looking men started yelling at us, trying to grab our attention. Wearing mismatched layers of clothes covered with holes and sporting dirty, overgrown beards, the men appeared to be homeless. They yelled over to us, "We gave the boy two dollars. It was all we had. He was great!" I was touched. I knew this was money they had earned panhandling.

One of them pointed to the guitar Justin had slung over his shoulder. "Can you play that?"

Justin and I nodded, still making our way through the crowd. I squeezed Justin's hand a little tighter and grabbed ahold of Nathan.

The two men continued to follow us as we walked. One of them shouted again, "Can we hear you play?" Justin nodded, and we motioned for them to follow us. If Nathan hadn't been with us, I wouldn't have said yes. I didn't make it a habit to go anywhere with strangers.

The five of us walked farther down the block. Justin got comfortable on the curb and carefully placed the guitar on his lap. The two men beamed in delight, smelling like they hadn't showered in days. Justin didn't seem to notice their body odor or their dirty clothes. He was just happy he could make them smile.

The men crouched down on the empty street in front of Justin, eager to hear a private concert. I heard Justin play the familiar chords of a song we sang in church. I was surprised that out of all the songs he could have chosen, Justin played that particular one. With a passion that was different from the way he'd played the drums and pail just minutes earlier, he started singing "Waves of Grace" from the depths of his heart.

> The walls are high, the walls are strong
> I've been locked in this castle
> That I've built for far too long
> You have surrounded me, a sea on every side
> The cracks are forming and I've got nowhere to hide
>
> Now I see
> The walls I've built are falling
> And Your waves of grace are washing over me
>
> Lord, please reign in every part
> I give my life to You, I open up my heart
> I want to be like You, I want to seek Your face
> O Lord, please wash me in Your awesome waves
>   of grace

As my son sang, I watched the two hardened men, men who had seen enough trouble to somehow end up on the streets. I didn't know their stories. I didn't know how they came to live on the streets. I just knew that something about the song touched them in a deep place. I saw tears well up in the eyes of one man. He was embarrassed and walked away, just far enough that we wouldn't see him cry. His buddy was also crying, though he didn't seem to care if he had an audience. I was moved by their emotions, especially at the prompting of a nine-year-old boy.

132

When Justin strummed his last chord, he looked up, tears flooding his eyes. His voice cracked as he said, "Jesus loves you guys so much."

The men nodded. "We know, buddy, we know."

Justin then ran a few feet down the block and bought the two men something to eat with the money he made busking. When he hugged them goodbye he said, "God bless you."

On the drive home, Justin cried. "Why can't we take them home, Mom? I don't want them to live outside," he begged, huge tears flooding down his cheeks.

I put my arm around my little boy, my heart aching from the compassion coming from his heart. I was proud of him—not just proud of his talent but proud of the character that was starting to take shape in his heart.

Though I loved being a mom and I gave it my all, I still struggled with the depression I'd had since I was a teenager as well as extreme

Most survivors of sexual abuse struggle with post-traumatic stress disorder (PTSD). Symptoms include: nightmares, flashbacks, debilitating anxiety, physical reactions to reminders of the event (like sweating, feeling sick to your stomach, a pounding heart), difficulty sleeping, feeling on edge and irritable, depression, hopelessness, intense feelings of guilt, shame, new phobias.

Here are some ways to cope with PTSD:

- Surround yourself with supportive friends and family.
- Learn as much as you can about the disorder.
- Avoid drugs and alcohol.
- Talk about it to someone you trust. Don't ignore the problem. It won't go away on its own.
- Seek help immediately from a therapist who specializes in PTSD.

anxiety that had developed when I was around twenty-one years old. At one point, I was diagnosed with post-traumatic stress disorder caused by all the painful events that happened when I was younger.

Particularly when Justin was around nine to about twelve years old, there were periods of time when I was so depressed that I had to force myself off the couch to play board games with him. It was even hard to get out of bed some mornings. Oh, what I would have given to sleep all day. I tried to pull myself up by the bootstraps and suck it up as best as I could. Some days were better than others.

> Anxiety doesn't just affect adults. While it's a normal part of our emotional makeup, anxiety can become a problem when it starts to control someone's life. It affects 25 percent of teens 13 to 18.[19]

I suffered from debilitating anxiety, which was so bad I would get physical pains in my chest and throat. I remember countless times when I would curl up in a fetal position and rock back and forth, crying out to God and begging Him to take the anxiety away.

I tried medication after medication to find a good fit, but most of them gave me horrible mood swings. Over a period of about twelve years, I probably tried close to twenty or thirty different ones, but none worked as I'd hoped. Some at least worked for a little bit, relieving my anxiety temporarily.

Every time I filled a new prescription, I'd desperately wish that maybe this would be the one that would cure my anxiety. Relieve my depression. Make me into a better person, a new person who had more energy and less crippling anxiety. That it would remove that cloud that hung over my head. Though some meds helped for a while, none worked long-term. There was no such thing as a magic pill for me.

In spite of how I felt, though, I knew where my priorities should be. I provided. I still showed up. I was there for Justin when he needed me. I cleaned. I cooked (okay, Kraft mac and cheese counts, right?). I took whatever little energy I had and poured it into caring for Justin. And I held on to my faith during this time, gaining strength and courage from God. In fact, I truly believe that some of my deepest moments of faith came from this time. But it wasn't easy.

twelve

"Mom, there's a singing competition and I want to try out."
Twelve-year-old Justin had just come home from school
and thrown his bulging backpack on the yellow shag carpet in the
living room.

I immediately noticed Justin was still wearing his boots. A
glistening trail of dirty melting snow ran from the front door to
where he stood in the kitchen. *If I've told him once, I've told him
a hundred times . . .*

"Helloooo." Justin annoyingly snapped his fingers in front of
my face, trying to get my attention. "So what do you think? Can
I try out or not?"

*An audition? What on earth is he talking about? Is this about
soccer? No, wait, didn't he mention something about singing?*
"Tell me about it," I said.

Justin hopped up on the chair next to me, fiddling with the
papers that covered the table. "It's called Stratford Star. It's kinda
like *American Idol*. Once you pass the auditions, you sing every
week against other kids, and then judges vote you off and stuff
until there's only three left."

Sounded like a competition for older kids. Justin wasn't even a
teenager yet. "How old do you have to be?"

"Twelve to eighteen."

Wow. That was quite a range. I couldn't imagine a twelve-year-old competing with an eighteen-year-old. That's six more years of training, experience, and developing skill. I was actually surprised Justin even considered auditioning. Outside of busking on the streets of Stratford and Toronto purely for fun, he hadn't performed in front of an audience and certainly not onstage in front of judges. Not to mention that even though I knew he had a great voice and natural talent, he hadn't taken a single voice lesson in his life.

I wasn't thrilled, but looking at Justin's eager face and seeing how he was dying for me to say yes, I decided to give him my blessing—just not before I offered words of caution. I didn't want to set him up for failure.

"Justin, listen to me. I believe in you, and I know you can do anything. You're talented and smart. Whatever you choose to do, I know you'll be successful at it. I just want you to be aware of some realities." I shared with Justin my theatrical background as a little girl. "I can't tell you how many times I auditioned for school plays and even community performances. I would pour my heart and soul into the auditions. And many times I believed wholeheartedly I'd get the part I wanted. But if I didn't, I was devastated. It broke my heart."

Justin eagerly nodded, hopping off the chair to stand up.

"This is just an audition," I continued. "Whether or not you make it does not have any bearing on who you are or how talented you are."

Though Justin's eyes were locked with mine and he was paying attention, I was pretty sure he was rolling his eyes on the inside. *Yeah, yeah, yeah, Mom, I know. If I don't win, who cares? Yada yada yada.*

But I wasn't done yet. "And another thing. You have to remember, you're competing with people much older than you, as much as six years. That's a big difference, honey. I'm sure these contestants, especially the older ones, have been doing this for a while. It's probably not their first time. I'm sure they've had training and more experience and a ton of practice. You understand that, right?"

Justin stood there, impatiently anticipating my answer. "So that's a yes, Mom?"

I smiled. "Yes, Justin. You can try out."

"Yes!" he said, complete with a fist pump.

But I still had just a little bit more to say. "And one more thing."

This time Justin groaned out loud.

"You're going to do your best, and you're gonna be awesome. And don't worry, if you don't get in, we'll get you some singing lessons, we'll practice a ton, and we'll get 'em next year!"

Justin took off to hang with his buddies. I made a phone call to find out more information and was told the auditions started on December 19, less than two weeks away. Definitely not a ton of time.

> Staying inside your comfort zone can feel good, familiar, like that old T-shirt you can't bear to throw out. There are times, however, when you will need to stretch your limits. Try out for a new sport. Take a new class. Go on a mission trip. Write the poem you've been afraid to write. Try out for the school play.
>
> Don't be scared to do something that might feel unfamiliar or challenging at first. It'll increase your confidence.

Up to the day before his first audition, I prepared Justin the best I could. I had total faith in him. He obviously had talent oozing out of every pore in his body. I just wasn't sure he could hold his own against older kids who'd spent hundreds of hours practicing for this very moment.

We had barely two weeks before the auditions. We went into overdrive, asking my musician friends who loved and believed in

Justin to help us however they could. Even though my son was a natural, he still had a lot to learn. Every day after school, Justin and I would drive over and practice in the youth center (not the Bunker), which had opened its doors for any wannabe contestant who wanted to use their sound equipment and karaoke machine.

> You can't rely on raw talent alone. Hard work, training, persistence, and a ton of practice are what will take you to the next level.

My musician friends came with us a few times to teach Justin about the basics of performing—things like how to hold a microphone, how to develop stage presence, and how to sing and groove with the music so it looks natural, not awkward. While Justin had to learn about the basics, he didn't have to learn the "it" factor. I knew it. My friends knew it. People at the youth center who watched him practice knew it. Whatever "it" was, Justin had it.

My son practiced all the time, everywhere—in the car, in the shower, at his grandparents' house. Sometimes he even practiced on the hockey bench when he was waiting to get thrown into a game or before he'd run some drills. Justin wasn't even aware he was singing out loud most times. Once he was on the bench and his buddy whipped off his helmet. "Dude, you realize you're singing, right?"

Justin tirelessly prepared for his audition. He (and nine other competitors) impressed the judges enough to make it through the auditions. There would be three weekly performance days, on which the contestants would sing two or three songs a night, until the final three were chosen. Those remaining competitors would then sing for the final time on January 27, 2007.

Justin and I kicked it into high gear. Together we picked songs that showcased his unique sound—my son definitely had some soul in him—and that he enjoyed singing. It was important that he have fun. The songs we picked were so different—from "Angel" by Sarah McLachlan to "3 AM" by Matchbox Twenty to "Respect" by Aretha Franklin to Lil' Bow Wow's "Basketball." We had a bit of everything, from pop to country to R&B.

When Justin took the stage to sing "Angel" and I aimed the video camera in his direction, I was nervous, probably more than he was. I quickly scoped out the audience filled with kids and parents, contestants and supporters. I wasn't the only anxious one in the room. I could feel the nervous energy.

Justin grabbed hold of the mic at the sound of the first notes. He looked a little uncomfortable, at least not as comfortable as he would look a few performances later. And his outfit? Oh my goodness. Looking back, what were we thinking? We never thought to pick out clothes to match the style of song. There he was, singing this gorgeous melody wearing a huge sweatshirt, a baseball cap, and a pair of oversized sneakers, hip hop style. His outfit didn't go unnoticed. "Pay attention to what you're wearing," one judge suggested. "Your wardrobe reflects your song."

Once Justin started singing, however, his outfit was the furthest thing from anyone's mind. He sounded amazing. His powerful voice echoed throughout the auditorium that was so quiet you could hear a pin drop. As my little boy sang the soothing tune, my heart melted. I could barely hold up the video camera. Do you know how hard it is to record when tears are welling up in your eyes? I videotaped every performance. I hated watching Justin through the lens and the videos are proof. They're dark, shaky, and blurry. But hey, I got the footage.

Justin blew me away on this song, as he would every song he sang. I knew if the judges didn't move him through that round, I would be just as proud. I stared at my twelve-year-old son onstage as he ended his performance with the sound of applause ringing in his ears. His smile was as big as the auditorium. It was obvious—he belonged onstage. It was home.

The truth is, Justin surprised me. He was the only twelve-year-old, the youngest in the entire competition. So when he made it through,

I was ecstatic. My jock of a son, who had never had a singing lesson, who had a late start preparing for the contest, who didn't even know how to properly hold a microphone two weeks earlier, made it past the first round. I'll never forget when it was the first judge's turn to critique Justin's performance. She was so overcome with emotion and tears, she had to wait a turn so she could compose herself and ultimately tell him what a great job he had done.

The more Justin performed, the more his confidence grew. Even his outfits got better. And the audience started to fall in love with this adorable adolescent boy with the charming and contagious grin.

While some of the other contestants who remained in the competition week after week were better trained, had more experience, and were more polished, Justin had a raw talent that made his mistakes forgivable and sometimes even unnoticeable. The crowd certainly didn't seem to mind how young and inexperienced Justin was. They were just blown away by his natural confidence on stage.

The judges gushed after his performances, aside from the one constructive criticism to choose better outfits to match the song. They called him a "natural born performer" and "Mr. Personality" and told him to "never lose that soul passion."

And then there were the girls. There were always the girls. Not long after Justin's first audition, word started spreading like wildfire across town about this cute kid who could sing. I remember walking into the auditorium one week and noticing more commotion than usual at the entrance. The closer we got, the louder the screams. With ponytails whipping in the wind like lassoes, a pack of preteen girls jumped up and down, invisible springs strapped to their feet.

As Justin passed, they squealed. Some of them seemed almost embarrassed when they caught his eye, but when Justin smiled and waved and thanked them for coming, they screamed louder. There were only a handful of them, but I tell you what, they were loud. It's pretty funny how much noise a tiny group of girls can make; three of them can easily sound like ten.

By the final week, the audience had grown so much that there were only a few empty seats in the place. There were more girls. More screaming girls. The screaming girls started bringing home-made signs that read in bright glittery letters "I love you, Justin Bieber" and "I vote for Justin." What a taste of things to come. After one of his performances, one judge joked, "I've been play-ing for twenty-five years and I've never had girls coming up to me like this."

Before Justin took the stage and after he performed during the final round, the crowd would chant his name. Girls, mostly. Twenty or thirty of them. "Justin! Justin! Justin!" The chanting alternated with the screaming, voices so loud the judges had to plug their ears. I thought it was hilarious. But there wasn't a doubt in my mind—Justin was the crowd favorite. (I know, I'm a little biased.)

My mom and Bruce faithfully showed up to each of Justin's performances, as did Jeremy and our extended families (grand-parents, aunts, uncles, cousins—you name it, they were there). Unfortunately, Justin's grandmother Kate, Jeremy's mom, lived a five-hour plane ride away and wasn't able to come. She loved her grandson, and not being able to support him in person devastated her. Justin and I knew she felt left out. He adored Kate and wanted to somehow make her feel involved.

We were at the house one day, Justin preparing for the next day's competition. He was practicing when he stopped cold. The melody turned into a yell.

"Mom!"

I was washing the dishes and couldn't hear much outside the rush of running water. I was about to yell back, "What?" but Justin was too impatient.

"Mom!"

This time Justin barreled into the kitchen like a horse that broke out of the gate. I was so startled I almost dropped a drinking glass on the linoleum floor.

I turned toward him, the dishwater dripping on my jeans. "What's up, honey?"

"Can we put the videos of the competition on YouTube for Grandma Kate?"

And that's how Justin first got on YouTube. He didn't go online to be famous. He did it for his grandmother.

Because I was pretty good with technology, I was able to not only upload the videos but also tag them for the search engine in such a way that his grandmother and even other relatives and family friends could easily find them in the YouTube video jungle. I even set up a channel specifically for Justin's videos called "Kidrauhl." The name was spun from his dad's online screen name, "Lordrauhl."

Grandma Kate loved the fact she could watch Justin online. It made her feel special. She was so proud of her grandson, she left one of the very first comments: "Well done, Justin. Hope the other one will be posted too, with the standing O intact!" Ironically, his first comment was from a stranger: "This kid is awesome." Justin's cousin followed up with, "Yep, he's awesome. He will be famous. He's only 12 now . . ."

Justin made it to the final three. When the winners were to be announced at the end of the performances, Justin stood onstage with the two other girl contenstants. Being so young, he looked tiny, like a grasshopper in the land of giants. I knew if he didn't win, I'd be somewhat bummed, but the fact that he shared the stage with talented singers who'd had years of vocal lessons and coaching was a big deal in itself. I was proud of him. Proud that he took a chance to even audition and proud that he made it to the top three. Justin's cheering section of girls was screaming so loudly in support I was sure their voices would be gone by the end of the night. Family and friends joined the hysteria, keeping our fingers crossed and anxiously hoping that he would come in first place.

I know Justin was disappointed when sixteen-year-old Kristen Hawley was announced as the winner. But he knew not to be a sore loser. Whether he was playing hockey or soccer, I always taught him how to be a good sport. As the crowd cheered for Kristen and her face glowed, soaking in the win, Justin reached his hand out to hers. He firmly shook it and whispered, "Congratulations." That small gesture touched my heart. As confident and bold as he was as a competitor, he always gave respect where it was due.

I could feel his disappointment building as we chitchatted afterward with the crowd. Judges, friends, family, and random people came up to us, shaking Justin's hand and telling him how awesome he did, even if he didn't come home with first place. My son was polite, nodding and saying "Thank you," shrugging and smiling when others told him he could always try again next year.

> *"I never thought of losing, but now that it's happened, the only thing is to do it right. That's my obligation to all the people who believe in me. We all have to take defeats in life."*
>
> —Muhammad Ali

I knew he was putting on a brave front. He couldn't hide from his mother how upset he was. All mamas can tell what's really going on behind a mask. Justin was born with a fierce competitive streak. He loved to win—at everything—so losing crushed him. He had poured his heart and soul into the contest. And week after week Justin beat the odds. I knew it was only a matter of time before his bubble of disappointment would burst.

We drove home in silence. From the corner of my eye I could see the tears welling up. I knew that no matter how many times I told him I was proud of him, no matter how many times I told him he had done an amazing job, it wouldn't lessen how devastated he felt.

Justin was always hardest on himself. He's still that way today. If at the end of a concert, he doesn't feel like the performance was up to his exceptionally high standards—even though everyone else thought he did an outstanding job—he's miserable. Justin has always been a perfectionist and works hard to be the best, whether he's playing soccer or hockey or performing onstage in front of thousands of people.

What started as a way to connect with his grandmother turned into random strangers finding the videos and even making specific requests. Justin and I started recording a ton of videos of him singing all kinds of songs. But we didn't just make videos for YouTube. I have thousands of videos of Justin simply being silly. He would fool around and make crazy faces and sounds, beatbox, and even make up raps.

> While nobody is perfect, it is important to be your best. Whether you are studying for an exam, playing in the state finals, leading the volunteer committee, or finishing your last term paper, commit to working your hardest. Don't just do the bare minimum or barely get by. Be determined to give your all. Always strive for excellence.

I got a kick out of every performance Justin did—whether it was a song for his YouTube fans or him breakdancing to Michael Jackson in front of no one else but me. I love watching the old videos. Without professional lighting or sound, they're as raw and organic as they come. They remind me where he began. How the craziness all started.

I stayed awake many nights past midnight, a Tim Hortons coffee to my right and my laptop opened in front of me. While Justin slept, I was up monitoring the YouTube channel, uploading new videos, keeping track of stats, and checking comments to make sure they weren't offensive. Maintaining the channel took a lot of time and sometimes was exhausting (hello, sleepless nights!), but I loved it. I looked forward to it. It was something fun to do. Every time I posted a video, I would refresh the page every two seconds to see the new comments and the change in view count. Yeah, I was pretty obsessed.

Friends and family weren't the only ones watching Justin's videos. While comments came in pretty quickly after we posted the first video, they started pouring in over the next few weeks from people all over the world.

"Wow, dude. You're pretty good."

"Nice voice, you're so talented."

"Justin, you're amazing. Watching this makes me want to marry you, lol."

"He's going to change the world."

Freelance jobs designing websites were slow in coming, so I took a part-time job at Conestoga College doing administrative work. I was also still teaching some basic computer courses to senior citizens at nearby nursing homes and giving private home lessons. Whenever I had a break in the middle of showing sweet old ladies how to use social media to stay connected with their grandkids, I would check the YouTube channel. How many more comments did Justin get? What did they think of his new song? How many people had watched his video since last night?

When Justin would get home from school, I was a nonstop blabberfest, giving him a play-by-play update on the comments that people wrote. Eventually, I started to get on his nerves. I admit, it was hard for me to dial back my excitement, but Justin grew annoyed when it was all I talked about.

The success of his home music videos snowballed in the blink of an eye. Six months after Justin lost the Stratford Star competition, his YouTube popularity was so high, monitoring his channel was like having a part-time job. In the beginning, I had the extra time to sort through the negative comments from haters—and boy, some people who had never met Justin and didn't know anything about him had some awful things to say; I don't know how people

Not everyone is going to be your biggest fan. Some of you may even be the victim of cyber-bullying or the innocent target of the mean girl at school. Be strong and don't let negative, stupid, and hurtful comments affect you. Focus on the positive qualities you know you have and the people in your life who love and accept you for who you are.

can be that mean to anybody, let alone a child. But we got as many as a hundred comments a day, which made it impossible to keep track of every single one.

Soon enough, Justin was a You-Tube celebrity. That was enough for me. It was such a fun, entertaining, and exhilarating experience, I couldn't even imagine what it must be like for a real star. I didn't even want to imagine that kind of life.

Justin's popularity got to the point where it wasn't just random strangers who had something to say about his rising YouTube fame. A few nationally syndicated talk shows wanted him on their program. As honored as I felt, I was nowhere near ready to even consider those opportunities.

thirteen

I couldn't believe the number of emails Justin started getting
through the YouTube channel from managers and various record
label executives. So many people wanted to turn him into a star.
It was all very overwhelming. And strange. I was used to having
an inbox full of messages from fans commenting how cute Justin
was and how much they loved him.

This was different. So I ignored the messages. I didn't want my
son having anything to do with the music business. I was suspicious
of these people who wanted to manage Justin's career. I figured
they just wanted to use him to get rich. Isn't that how the industry
works? So thanks but no thanks. We're not interested.

I had no intention of showing the messages to Justin. The truth
was, I had a pipe dream that Justin was going to become a worship
leader or youth pastor. All my talented musician friends were worship leaders, so I just assumed Justin would do the same.

I was also hesitant because I was afraid. Everyone knows what
happens to many child artists. I had heard all the horror stories.
Almost a teenager, Justin would have plenty to deal with in high
school on his own. But when the emails about music careers kept
on coming, I realized I had to look outside my bubble. As a praying
mother, I did just that—I prayed about the opportunities.

When Justin was a baby, I dedicated his life to God in a special ceremony at my church, much the same way that Hannah dedicated Samuel in the Bible (see 1 Sam. 1). That day I prayed and asked God to raise Justin up to be a leader and a voice to his generation.

This story came to mind as I was praying about Justin's future one evening. I felt God telling me to trust Him. To let go of my plans for Justin. It was time for me to stop figuring out Justin's future for him. And that's when I finally started paying attention to the emails and calls coming in. I even considered the possibility that God could be the one opening those very doors.

In the middle of 2007, a manager from Atlanta named Scooter went to crazy lengths to try to contact me. He was relentless. He sent emails to me through the YouTube channel. He tried to get through to other people who he hoped would get in contact with me for him. This guy messaged one of my top friends on MySpace, called Justin's great-aunt whom my son had never met (in addition to anyone with the last name Bieber where we lived), and tried to get in touch with me via the Avon Theatre, the place in the YouTube video where he had watched Justin sing. All these people called me and left message after message that some young guy named Scooter with a Gmail address was trying to reach me about Justin. Probably one of Scooter's boldest moves was when he called Justin's school by way of the Stratford Board of Education.

> Sometimes the plans we have for our lives are not necessarily the ones that are destined for us. It reminds me of the quote, "If you want to make God laugh, tell Him your plans." Maybe it's time for you to look outside your own bubble.

I didn't know much about this guy other than what I was told from the people in my life he was contacting. I knew his name was Scooter Braun. He had name-dropped popular music stars, so I knew he'd worked with famous artists like Usher, Justin Timberlake, and Britney Spears. I also knew he had a Gmail address.

I wasn't impressed by name-dropping. I'd heard it all before from other managers and so-called record execs who promised they had worked with or were friends with this or that famous person. It was usually far from the truth.

Scooter's Gmail address also made me suspicious. Why wouldn't he have an email address with his record label name? All the other emails I got came from reputable management groups, like joeschmoe@so-and-so-company.

I admired his persistence, but I didn't take Scooter's efforts seriously. I finally called him just to get him to leave me and everyone he was calling alone. I used a computer line so I could block my name and number. No need to give him a direct channel to reach me.

> Anyone—a boyfriend, a sibling, a friend, someone who is trying to convince you to do something—can promise you the moon and the stars. Don't believe everything you hear. Be cautious. Be smart. Don't be pressured into doing something you don't want to or are not ready to do just because you are promised the world.

I was exhausted from teaching computer classes that afternoon. My feet hurt from standing for hours, and all I had eaten the entire day was a stale bagel. I only planned for a five-minute conversation with Scooter. I didn't have much to say other than "Please stop calling." I had more important things to do, like taking a long, hot bubble bath.

I dialed Scooter's number, but my mind was on my much-needed R and R.

"This is Scooter."

"Hi," I said in a flat tone of voice. "This is Pattie Mallette, Justin Bieber's mom."

"Ms. Mallette, thank you so much for calling me back!" Scooter couldn't hide his excitement if he tried.

I started right into my planned "thanks but no thanks" speech, looking at my watch to see what time it was. Before I knew it, two hours had passed. We chatted away like long-lost friends.

Scooter told me how he found Justin on YouTube and how my son's talent blew him away. Then he told me about himself, what exactly he did for a living. "Just google me," he suggested. "You can find out information about some of the projects I've done and people I've worked with."

While Scooter was definitely a fast and smooth talker—hey, it's what he does for a living—something about him seemed genuine and warm. The conversation took off in all sorts of interesting directions. Scooter and I talked about everything from Justin and his potential career in the music industry to our faith.

Scooter ended the conversation by inviting us to meet him in Atlanta. "I'll introduce you to some people down here so you can see for yourself that I'm legit, that I'm not blowing smoke. You don't have to sign anything. You don't have to promise to do anything. No pressure. No obligations. If you come and you hate it, consider this a free paid vacation to Atlanta. At least think about it."

As persistent as Scooter was, he never pressured me into anything. I was always honest about any fears I had, and Scooter understood my suspicions about the music industry. So sure, of course I could think about meeting him.

I took time to pray after that phone call. I didn't even mention it to Justin yet; I still had a lot of thinking to do. I also wanted to hear what God's best was.

At the time Jeremy lived in Winnipeg, twelve hundred miles away from Stratford. Though he and Justin didn't see each other regularly, simply because of the distance, Jeremy and I had conversations during this time. Just as I was, he was both happy and worried sick about the potential opportunity.

It's super important to have wise adults in your life who you respect, trust, and can talk to. Sometimes you need guidance from someone older, with more life experience, and who has your best interest at heart. Whether it's a teacher, a counselor, a parent, or even a friend's parent, don't be afraid to ask them for advice if you have an important decision to make. In Proverbs 11:14, the Bible tells us that wisdom is found in a multitude of counselors.

After Scooter's offer, I talked to John and Sue as well as other spiritual leaders at my church whom I trusted. As much as I tried to convince my mentors it was probably best not to move forward, every one of them felt a peace about it.

Everyone except me. I was thankful for their support, but it still wasn't enough for me.

———————

After much praying, thinking, and seeking counsel from wise leaders, I decided I would consider Scooter's offer on two conditions. I prayed for confirmation that Scooter was supposed to be Justin's manager and that I would find an entertainment attorney. I didn't want to even consider meeting with Scooter unless we had legit representation. I had been warned by a friend who had been burned; she strongly urged me to get a good attorney. The fact was, I didn't know a thing about contracts, negotiations, or anything relating to the music business. I didn't want to get cornered.

Finding a lawyer seemed impossible, at least in my eyes. I barely had enough money to put food on the table. I'd heard a good one cost up to $900 an hour. Are you kidding me? That year I barely made $10,000 between all the jobs I worked. I couldn't come up with $900 in a month! I would have to either win the lottery or find an attorney who would work with us for free. None of those options looked likely.

It wasn't long before one of my prayers was answered. Scooter called one day to see if I had been thinking about his offer and how I felt about visiting with him.

I was up-front and told him my concerns. Scooter didn't hesitate a half a second and told me he'd make some phone calls. He had connections with some bigwig lawyers who didn't require any money up front. A few days later, I got a call from one of the top entertainment lawyers in the business, who agreed to take Justin on as a client. He was exactly what I had in mind.

I was shocked. There it was, one answer to my prayer, right before my eyes. When I had thought of the idea of possibly having a top entertainment lawyer to give us advice, it sounded crazy. I never imagined it would actually happen. But somehow, it did. So far so good.

I still had to talk to Justin before confirming the trip to meet with Scooter. The topic was a big deal. We were thinking about things that could change his life. Surprisingly, it was one of the easiest conversations I've ever had with him.

I had just come home from work, ready to change into a pair of comfy sweats. I sank into my favorite spot on the living room couch and opened Justin's YouTube page.

As I started eyeballing the new emails that had come in the last few hours, I heard the key jiggle in the front door. "Hey, Mom, what's up?" Justin barreled through the apartment and made his way over to me wearing a backward baseball cap and a hoodie. He looked like he was coming home only to go right back out. He was always busy doing something—playing sports, going to the skate park, playing video games at his friend's house. If he wasn't singing and I wasn't holding a video camera, it was like pulling teeth to get him to sit with me and talk. He was the same two-year-old boy with wild energy, a toddler always on the move.

"Sit with me for a minute, Justin. I want to talk to you about something."

Justin plunked down on the couch, leaning in to give me a kiss on the cheek.

I took a deep breath and chose my words carefully. I didn't want Justin to feel I was pressuring him at all. "Do you like singing?"

"Um, yeah."

"Do you love singing?"

"Sure."

"What do you want to be when you grow up, Justin?"

"A professional hockey or soccer player, probably. I don't know. Why?" He started fiddling with his shoelaces.

"Okay. Now, if you had the opportunity to sing and play music as a career, would you do it? Or even think about it?"

Justin sighed, annoyed at my nonstop questioning. I wonder if he had a clue where I was going with all this. "Yeah, probably. Why are you asking me all these questions?"

I wanted him to understand—and I wasn't sure if he did—that the decision I was going to ask him to make wasn't a joke or something we could afford to take lightly, like picking out a new pair of jeans.

"Well, we have the opportunity to go to Atlanta to meet with some people and check it out. What do you think about that? You want to give it a shot?"

I closed my eyes, almost hoping he wouldn't be interested so we could call it a day and forget about this whole music business stuff.

But Justin didn't say no. His eyes lit up. He said, "Yeah, sure! When do we get to go?"

I set up a Skype call with Scooter. I wasn't going to make the two-hour flight without Justin first meeting Scooter. The two of them hit it off immediately. Scooter's young at heart, fun, and great

Making a decision isn't always easy. The hardest choices, of course, are those that will affect your future. How can you make the best decisions? Here are some ideas that will help you.

Do the research. Think about your options. Talk to people who have been in similar situations. Consider the consequences of your decision. What are the pluses and the minuses? How will it affect you in the long-term? Seek advice from wise and trusted mentors. And most importantly, pray about it.

with kids, and Justin quickly took to him. It was settled. Though I wasn't going to make any decisions about Scooter until I got my final confirmation, we were going to Atlanta.

All systems were go, but I still wondered about my prayer to know without a doubt that Scooter was meant to be Justin's manager. From the outside, he seemed like a pretty good guy who knew what he was doing. But still, I needed to know for sure.

A few days before our trip, I was running an errand downtown.

"Hey, Pattie," I heard someone call out. I turned around and saw my friend Nathan. He was walking with a young man I didn't know. The guy he was with was looking at me weird. Not in a creepy way, though. It almost seemed like he wanted to say something but kept choking back the words. Finally he said, "I'm not sure how this is going to sound or if you're going to think this is crazy, but I really believe I have a word from God for you."

My heart started pounding. "Sure, let me have it," I answered.

"I feel like you have been thinking or praying about working with a Jewish man. And I feel like God is saying 'yes, yes, and yes.' The favor of God is on him. God blesses everything this man touches."

Scooter was Jewish, and although I didn't have any problem with that, I also had originally thought Justin would be part of the Christian music world. I was in awe. It couldn't have been any clearer. Someone I had never met was telling me the answer to my prayer.

"Wow! Thanks! You are right on. I've been praying about this very thing." I marveled at how God can operate in the strangest of places, in the strangest of ways, and through the lives of perfect strangers. We spoke for a few minutes, and I shared with them about the potential opportunity that was awaiting Justin and how reluctant I had been to pursue it.

I had just received confirmation from a total stranger who didn't know anything about me, my son, or our situation. It was official. I knew that at least for this season, Scooter was the right choice. I knew he would be the one who would play a significant role in Justin's life and music career. I was excited but somewhat nervous. I hadn't a clue what lay ahead. I hadn't a clue what doors our trip to Atlanta would open. Frankly, I would never have even imagined the possibilities in my wildest dreams.

fourteen

Justin and I boarded the plane for our two-hour-plus flight to Atlanta. Right before we stepped into the aisle to make our way to our seats, a pretty flight attendant tapped Justin on the shoulder. "Would you like a tour of the cockpit?" she asked, winking discreetly at me. "We're not really allowed to do this, but the captain said you can come and check it out." Only moments earlier, I had mentioned to one of the crew that it was Justin's first time on a plane.

As the rest of the passengers squeezed past us, Justin exploded in a mile-wide smile. "Sure!"

Surrounded by buttons, switches, and flashing lights, Justin listened intently to the captain and co-pilot's quick overview of the flight systems. He didn't say much except "Cool" and "No way!" I rummaged through my purse to find a camera, the one I'd have glued to my hand the entire trip, and snapped a photo of Justin. My son grinned with one hand clutching the airplane throttle. His long, dirty-blond hair peeked through the oversized hat the pilot was kind enough to let him wear. I had a feeling being able to tour the cockpit was the beginning of many firsts for Justin on this trip.

As the roar of the engines sounded when the plane started down the runway, Justin pressed his face against the window. We started picking up speed, the jet rumbling louder. The nose of the airplane began to lift, gently pushing us back into our seats. Justin was thunderstruck. "We're going! We're going! We're going! We're almost there!" The plane continued to rise, the last touch of the wheels grazing the runway. Hit with a sinking feeling in his belly as we soared into the open blue sky, Justin moaned, "Oh, my stomach. My stomach is like, bleahh!" But he quickly recovered, staring out the window as the city below became smaller and smaller. "This is awesome," Justin burst out. "I can see everything!"

We finally touched down in Atlanta and made our way through the busiest airport in the United States with butterflies in our stomachs. Justin had the same curious look as when we roamed the streets of downtown Toronto when he was six. But he wasn't a little kid anymore; he was a teenager. Too old to hold my hand as we rushed through the midday crowd in the terminal, but still young enough that he needed me (though as a typical teenager, he probably wouldn't admit it).

I sighed. *He's growing up too fast.*

"C'mon, Mom, let's go!" Justin snapped me back to reality.

"I'm coming, I'm coming," I muttered, playfully annoyed.

We made it through to the baggage claim area, calling Scooter as we walked to tell him we had arrived.

"Awesome! Look for the purple Mercedes out front," he told us. "You can't miss it."

We saw Scooter as soon as we walked out of the terminal. He flashed a winning smile when he hopped out of his car to grab our bags. He gave me a warm hug and high-fived Justin. "It's so good to see you guys. How was your flight?"

As we sped off toward downtown Atlanta, whizzing down the highway, Scooter told us of his plans. "I just got a call from Jermaine Dupri. He challenged me to a video game at the studio, NBA 2K8. You guys mind if we stop in for a bit?"

Justin piped up from the backseat. "Oh, I love that game! Can I play with you guys?"

Scooter looked at Justin in the rearview mirror. "Of course." He smiled slyly. "But be prepared to lose."

It was game on for Justin. He wasn't one to pass up a friendly competition. Scooter and Justin smack talked the entire way.

I loved how the two of them immediately hit it off. Scooter was silly and always made Justin laugh, especially when he broke out in his "surfer dude" voice. I was quiet, just watching the two of them interact, trying to read Scooter as best as I could.

I couldn't be distracted. I had to focus on being Justin's mom and determining the best for his future. I couldn't get caught up in the glamour of him possibly being a music artist. I just had to sit back and observe. By then, I didn't doubt that Scooter was successful and had accomplished some big things. So while I respected him, I was on guard for Justin's sake.

Right when we pulled up to the studio, a black Range Rover pulled up alongside us. When Justin saw who got out of the truck, he practically cannonballed out of the backseat. Dressed in a leather jacket and wearing designer shades, Usher swaggered past us into the studio.

"Hey, Usher," Justin called out, trying to catch up with one of his music heroes. "I'm a huge fan and I know your songs. Can I sing you one?"

Usher smiled and politely brushed us off. "Some other time, buddy. It's cold outside." We wouldn't see him again until our next trip a few months later.

Scooter asked if I could wait in the lobby while he and Justin went inside the studio. Of course I could. But I'll be honest. Though I knew it wasn't personal, I was disappointed. I knew Scooter wanted to play it cool and not make a big deal out of Justin meeting Jermaine (I think he even may have introduced Justin as his nephew). But it made me feel left out.

Here I was, a mother who had spent the last thirteen years single-handedly raising her son. It had been us against the world. And now we were in another country, facing some important decisions, and we were apart. I never liked being away from Justin, and I don't even now. I walked around the lobby while I waited, trying to keep myself busy. There were plaques lining the wall showing off platinum and gold records from artists like Mariah Carey and Destiny's Child. Pretty cool, I thought, but I still wasn't sold.

> Your values—what you believe is or is not important—are a big deal. Whether you know it or not, they play a huge part in the small and big decisions you make every day. Your values influence things like who you hang out with, how you spend your time, how you treat people, and how you choose to live your life.

Later that day, Scooter took us to his friend's high-rise apartment, where we would stay for the week. The minute we walked into the posh pad on the thirty-second floor, I felt I was inside the pages of a luxury interior design magazine. The place was stylish and sleek. It boasted shiny hardwood floors, a white plush rug at the foot of a candy apple red leather couch, floor-to-ceiling windows with stunning views of downtown, and Justin's all-time favorite, the biggest flat-screen TV he had ever seen. The bedrooms were stark white and had little in them except for more flat-screen TVs and the most comfortable beds we'd ever slept in. Justin and I had died and gone to *MTV Cribs* heaven.

In between our meetings with different producers and singers, Scooter got a call one day from his dad, who lived in Connecticut. He was on his way home and had a layover in Atlanta. Scooter hoped the four of us could meet at the airport before his dad's flight home.

Before we ever met in person, Scooter had said great things about his parents and how family values and morals were important to him. I was looking forward to meeting with his dad to get an idea of Scooter's upbringing. If Scooter was going to be Justin's manager and a huge influence in his life, I wanted to be sure he was a man of integrity. And what better way to find out than by meeting his father?

Ervin Braun, a successful dentist, met us at the food court. I think he had just come back from a wakeboarding trip. A tall, handsome man, he had an unmistakable presence, confident but not cocky. He was also down-to-earth, one of the nicest men I've ever met. At one point Scooter walked his dad over to a quiet hallway so Justin could sing for him. Ervin enjoyed the private performance.

Over deli sandwiches, I asked Scooter's dad question after question, repeating my fears and concerns about Justin being in the entertainment industry. He stressed that his son was trustworthy, had integrity, and would take great care of us. I know Ervin wasn't trying to play us. Every word was sincere. I had pretty good gut instincts; I just knew it.

But I also watched Scooter and his dad in action. It was obvious they not only loved each other but had a mutual respect and the same values. I was impressed by their relationship. I knew Scooter came from a good family, and meeting Ervin helped me eventually seal the deal.

> **"Quick decisions are unsafe decisions."**
>
> —Sophocles

We left Atlanta without making any official commitments. Justin was still in school, and I didn't want to take him out before the year was over. While I wasn't ready to rush into anything, Justin was locked and loaded. If it were up to him, we would have signed on the dotted line before we headed back to Canada. I told Scooter we'd be in touch to discuss what it would look like if we did decide to move forward with him as Justin's manager.

I was honest with Justin, encouraging him and giving him a reality check at the same time. "I know all of this is amazing," I told him. "But don't get your hopes up. I haven't decided anything yet."

Even though I had confirmations to my two biggest questions, I was still unsure. Especially about moving from Canada to Atlanta. There was so much at stake, and it wasn't about me. This was about Justin, my only child. I needed a little more time before I took the leap and uprooted our lives to another country.

———————

Two or three weeks after our trip to Atlanta, I finally made the official decision. I called Scooter—we were moving to Atlanta. He started drawing up the contracts.

I was thrilled for Justin, excited to see how this new chapter in his life would unfold. Of course, I still had my concerns about the unpredictability of the music industry and the scary reality of what can happen to young artists. After Scooter officially became Justin's manager, it was time to plan our move to the United States.

We are much more than our talents, our looks, our abilities, our athletic skills, and our smarts. Sure, those things help make up who we are, but they are not our identity. Gifts come from above, and we are blessed to receive them.

I had plenty of serious talks with Justin during this time. I continued to encourage him, always quick to tell him how proud I was. But at the same time, I didn't want him to get an inflated ego. I always reminded him where his gifts came from and how he found himself surrounded by incredible opportunities. As a mother, I needed to make sure I gave him a balanced perspective. Yes, he was talented, but his talent came from God, not himself.

Many times, in different ways, I warned Justin, "You can take credit for being disciplined and working hard to hone your talents, but you can't take credit for being naturally good at them. God gave you these gifts. And the only reason you're in this position is because of Him."

Though I never shoved my faith down Justin's throat, I gave him a strong foundation. I taught him faith values knowing he would have to make the choice how to live his life and what paths he would follow. It will always be his choice.

Though Justin was still in school and I didn't plan on taking him out until the year was over, he was beside himself. Meanwhile, life continued its steady pace back in Stratford. I worked, Justin went to school, and we posted videos online. That was pretty much it.

Scooter and I worked together to build up Justin's YouTube following. We stayed up endless nights monitoring the channel, posting videos, and watching his popularity grow. A few record labels were interested in Justin, but there were no serious bites until Scooter brought in Usher and Justin Timberlake. It was an honor just to be considered by both artists. Though we ultimately decided to work with Usher, I feel that we wouldn't have lost either way.

I remember the short trip to see Usher in February 2008. Justin was stoked to meet one of his idols. I admit, I was pretty excited myself. I grew up listening to his music and admired him. Usher met us at what looked like a dance studio. A mirror lined one wall and chairs were scattered about. Justin did his thing, singing songs like "I'll Be" by Edwin McCain and even Usher's "U Got It Bad." In the middle of a riff in the latter song, Justin playfully asked Usher, "You gonna sing with me or what?" and kept right on singing. He wasn't nervous. Not one bit. A natural performer, Justin never gets nervous.

Justin and Usher hit it off. They were both competitive. Usher's favorite game was Connect Four, and Justin mentioned he hadn't played in a while. At one or two in the morning, hours before we were scheduled to fly back to Canada, Usher had a Connect Four game and a Rubik's Cube dropped off for Justin. We were touched by the sweet gesture. And Justin was itching to practice so he could play Usher one day and beat him.

When I shared with my parents the news about moving to Atlanta after the school year, they were excited. They understood that Justin had an opportunity to do great things. Like any grandparents would be, though, they were also heartbroken that their grandson would be eight hundred miles away. Bruce was crushed. He and Justin shared a special bond.

I had never seen Bruce shed a tear until Justin performed in the Stratford Star contest. He had a soft spot in his heart for his grandson. When we told him and my mom about our decision to move, Bruce was a blubbering mess. He was going to miss his little boy. The two of them were a team. Every Friday night, he and Justin would watch the local hockey game at the Allman Arena. Bruce also came with me to every one of Justin's hockey games and even took him to most of his practices.

I knew the entertainment world had its share of dangers and temptations, but I also knew Justin would be better protected in Atlanta than in high school back home. Without being around Justin 24/7 in Stratford, known on the streets as the "meth capital" of Canada, I wouldn't know what kind of trouble he could get into, and believe me, even though it was a small city, there was a lot of trouble around.

From the start, Scooter and I were careful to choose the right people to work with and be around Justin. Though we may not agree on everything, Scooter and I have the same commitment to protecting Justin. We never surrounded him with "yes" men or women. We wanted people on his team who would challenge his character and encourage his integrity. So while I was anxious about the move, I also felt confident about my son's well-being. Scooter and I would always know where Justin was and what he was up to.

As I scrambled to end one chapter of our life and begin a new one, it took time for reality to set in. Once it did, I had to say goodbye to the familiar and say hello to the unknown. It was pretty scary.

The last month before I moved out of my apartment was full of tears. Lots of tears. The days merged into one another as I prepared to leave my hometown, the only place I had ever known as home. I took long drives on miles of empty roads alongside picturesque farms on the outskirts of the city. I drove through the charming streets of downtown Stratford, past the library where Justin and I had read countless books like *Clifford the Big Red Dog* and the Arthur series. I drove past old neighborhoods, remembering good times with old friends.

I was leaving behind places and things that gave me comfort, that made me laugh. Everything I had loved about Stratford—from the beautiful river where my son and I admired graceful swans and fed quacking ducks to the theater stage I had performed on and called my second home to the homey diners and cafés where my best friends and I would spend hours talking—would be mere memories, eight hundred miles away from my new hometown of Atlanta, Georgia.

> Change can be difficult or fantastic, but one thing is certain: change is inevitable. When life happens and you are faced with a major change—your parents get divorced, you have to move, you have a new teacher—take the time to really feel your emotions. Then take things one day at a time as you adjust to the newness.

As soon as I gave my landlord notice, my mom swept in like an army general. She started to get rid of my stuff. We couldn't take much to Atlanta—only whatever could fit in a suitcase or two.

Everything was happening way too fast. In the time it takes to blink—at least that's how it felt—I found myself a week or two before the move, living in an apartment furnished only with a mattress in the middle of the living room. A handful of Justin's clothes were thrown in one corner, and a few outfits of mine hung in the closet. The apartment wasn't the only thing that was empty. I was too.

Before my apartment was stripped bare, I had a lot of cleaning to do. I'll never forget one time when I walked around holding an overstuffed trash bag in one hand. I filled it with old, broken toys that Justin had stopped playing with years ago. Tears fell. Again. He wasn't a baby anymore. He wasn't even a little kid. Justin was growing up and literally going to strange places where I didn't have a map to help him find his way through. It seemed like just yesterday when Justin was banging on his high chair, playing the drums for the first time. Was it really over ten years later?

I would stand alone in the empty apartment on moving day, surrounded by the awful off-white walls that looked permanently dirty. I gazed around the rooms—past the kitchen counter I could never get clean enough, the old appliances that were falling apart, the many nicks and scratches on the walls. Though my head spun from a dozen emotions, I felt sure about one thing: I was definitely not going to miss this dingy apartment.

As my friend Scott, a lifesaver in those last few weeks, helped move some of the heavier things out to the garbage dump one day, I crumpled into his arms like a rag doll. I sobbed on his shoulders. Though a new chapter was about to be written, I felt my very life, the one I had built, slipping away from my fingers. When we walked out toward the end of the street, from the corner of my eye, I could see the local convenience store where Justin got slushies almost every day after school. Another round of tears fell, turning Scott's white T-shirt into a wet mess.

Scott took me, Justin, and one of Justin's best friends, Chaz, camping at Pinery Provincial Park a week before we left for Atlanta. It helped to take some of the edge off. For a few days, we hiked while we swatted away annoying mosquitoes in the afternoon humidity. We cooled off in the calm, clear waters of the lake and played on the wide sand dunes. Justin and Chaz spent hours building tiny teepee fires. At night, we huddled in our sleeping bags in a cozy tent, falling asleep under the moonlight to the sound of chirping crickets.

We had a great time together. And that was the point. I wanted to give Justin one last fun adventure. I wanted him to spend time with his best friend and not have to think about the next new phase in his life and leaving behind all he had ever known.

> Saying goodbye is never easy. In those moments, we need to hold on to the memories, which will last a lifetime.

As the countdown to moving got closer to the actual day, I threw Justin a huge going-away party on our friend Chad's farm. From what I saw, it looked like every student from his middle school was there. Some played volleyball or rode quads, and others hung out by the long buffet table. When the sun set, the teenagers gathered around a huge bonfire and sang songs, led by Justin on his guitar. He even busted out solos, singing songs like "Cry Me a River" by Justin Timberlake. The party ended with a display of colorful fireworks.

My own going-away party was nowhere near as big or elaborate. I invited about fifty people I knew. Only nine showed up, including John's wife, Sue, and their daughter, Tasha. Though I was disappointed in the low turnout, we had a blast. It was my first time at a country western lounge. We tore up the dance floor, stomping our way through dance steps we didn't know while banjos and fiddles blared through the speakers.

The night before we left, Justin and I spent a few hours driving around town. It was our turn to say goodbye together. We didn't talk much but blasted the stereo as we always did. As the schools Justin attended, the skate park he frequented, and the parks we had explored faded from our view, we finally said goodbye.

fifteen

Moving to Atlanta marked a new beginning. Though I was grateful for the fresh start, I felt caught in an emotional spider web—feeling homesick, eager for the new adventure, and nervous about what lay ahead.

I believed in Justin with all my heart and was excited for his new future. I knew without a doubt how talented he was and how badly he wanted this. I just didn't know what to expect, especially coming from a small town in Canada. Stratford has a population of thirty thousand people and one of the lowest crime rates in all of Canada. Atlanta, home to over five million people, is one of the most dangerous cities in the United States, with a crime rate five times the national average. That's a big difference.

Scooter warned us he would be gone the first week after our move. He didn't mean for it to happen; it was just bad timing. The day we

> "Settling into a new country is like getting used to a new pair of shoes. At first they pinch a little, but you like the way they look, so you carry on. The longer you have them, the more comfortable they become."
>
> —Tahir Shah, *In Arabian Nights*

arrived in Atlanta was like a fog. Scooter dropped us off at a hotel in Buckhead, gave us three hundred bucks for the week, and took off on a business trip.

The area where we stayed was breathtaking. The hotel was nestled in one of the wealthiest areas in Atlanta. We were surrounded by luscious landscaping, surprisingly clean streets, and glitzy stores too pricey to even window-shop. Everything was so expensive, we couldn't really do much. I certainly wasn't going to pay twenty bucks for a hamburger or seventy-five dollars a ticket to see a show. Besides, Justin and I were in an unfamiliar area. I didn't feel safe exploring on our own.

The stress of moving, being alone, and not knowing anyone took a toll on me not long after we arrived. The first week was naturally overwhelming. My head exploded in a migraine. Looking back, I feel terrible for Justin. The pain was so bad, all I could do was lay in bed all day. My poor son went stir crazy in our small hotel room. We fought a lot. It was almost impossible not to.

Kenny Hamilton, Scooter's good friend who would end up being one of Justin's bodyguards, showed up at our hotel room one day and rescued my son. He took Justin out a few times that week while I nursed my migraine, huddled under hotel sheets trying not to move. I'll never forget Kenny's kindness that week—and to this day.

A week later, Scooter was back, and we spent a few nights at his girlfriend's parents' house. Finally it was time to go home—our new home tucked away in a quiet community in the middle of the city. The three-story townhouse was beautiful. Just walking through the front doors brought me peace. The place was empty. Everything looked new and clean, nothing at all like my old apartment. *Hello, home.*

The three of us drove to a furniture store where Scooter paid for a bunch of used couches, tables, and bedroom sets. We also went to Target and loaded up two carts with every household item imaginable—toilet paper, dishes, towels, pots, pans, sheets, clocks, and toiletries. Our final stop was a grocery store. I've never bought so much food at once in my life (thanks, Scooter!). We stocked our fridge and pantry with condiments, cereal, pasta, fruits, vegetables, snacks, soda, and juices. As a single mother who had spent the last thirteen years counting pennies, I felt like we had won the lottery. Setting up house was really fun.

Still, leaving everything and everyone we knew was really hard on me because we didn't know anyone outside of Scooter and Kenny. We didn't have a church yet or a network of support. Even the friends I had back home seemed to be too busy to connect. I missed home so much it physically hurt. I cried for six months.

During that time, the debilitating depression and anxiety came back in full force. Not finding a church I could call home was tough. It made me feel lonelier, especially on Sundays when I would sit in unfamiliar buildings for two hours surrounded by people I didn't know.

> When you're away from your friends and those you love, you realize how much you need them. Having people around who love you, believe in you, and are rooting for you is important to having a healthy life, especially when you are experiencing a major change. Don't ever take your friends or your loved ones for granted.

I developed crazy fears, like being afraid of flying (which wasn't a good fear to develop since we were flying often). I also had nightmares. Though I struggled with my loneliness and the stresses that come from moving to another country, I knew I had to hold on to my faith.

In the midst of the darkness, there were moments I was encouraged by a message, an old friend's heartfelt prayer, or feeling the presence of God in a way I hadn't experienced in a while. I held on to those moments for dear life.

Over time, the darkness began to lift. I felt less and less anxious. The depression quieted down. All of the fears and phobias that I had suddenly developed vanished. And after a few months, I found a church and a handful of wonderful people who could support me spiritually and encourage and pray for me when I needed it.

I think I was an emotional wreck because of the extreme change. I had to dig deep with God during this time. It challenged me to cope with my faith on my own, and in fact, strengthened it. Extreme change would become my new normal as we entered the fast-paced life of nonstop travel and spending time in a different hotel room every night.

> *"When a train goes through a tunnel and it gets dark, you don't throw away the ticket and jump off. You sit still and trust the engineer."*
>
> —Corrie ten Boom

Things were happening so big and so fast for Justin. Between watching him record and traveling with him doing radio promos all over the country, I was responsible for signing contracts that could affect Justin's future. I had to review pages and pages of legal mumbo jumbo, and even though I had an attorney to help me, it was still a challenge. At the end of the day, I was Justin's mother. I was responsible for any consequences that could come from any document I signed or deal I made possible.

There were times I was overcome with fear. I was afraid of making a mistake. I felt so much pressure. What if I signed something that could steer Justin in the wrong direction?

But I couldn't allow those questions and fears to control me. I know God wouldn't have put me in this situation to make me fail or fall. I began to listen to my instincts and follow the peace in my heart. And I constantly reminded God that He was the one who told me to trust Him. I'm sure I made mistakes along the way, but what parent doesn't?

174

The rest of the story is history. Most of you know it well: The platinum-selling albums. The multiple Billboard hits. The world-wide number-one singles. The Grammy Awards. The American Music Awards. The world tours. The fans. The absolutely amazing fans like you.

I'm so proud of Justin. I'm in awe of how far he has come and how tirelessly he works to entertain his fans. One thing I've always admired about my son is his ability to switch from Justin Bieber the performer to Justin Bieber the normal teenager. From the start he didn't allow the cameras, the hype, the screaming fans, the glitz, or the glamour to turn him into a different person.

I remember the time Justin opened for Taylor Swift. This was his first big performance. By this time he had done small shows and appearances during his radio promo tour all over the country, but nothing at all like this. This was his breakout moment. Justin had a giant online following at this point—nothing close to what he has now, of course—and the publicity for the major event was off the hook. Thousands of concertgoers filled the massive stadium. Pops of lights flashed. The thunderous roar of screaming girls made it impossible to even think.

I was nervous for my son, anxiously pacing around backstage in the company of Scooter and Ryan (Justin's road manager/stylist who traveled with us everywhere). I had a gnawing feeling in the pit of my stomach. I was sure Justin would spend the last moments before he had to go onstage having some quiet time alone, needing to rehearse and focus. I wanted to give Justin a pep talk, to remind him to relax and that he'd do great. I was sure he would need some encouragement from his mama.

Ready to wrap my arms around him in a warm hug just moments before his performance, I couldn't believe what I saw when I found him backstage. He was huddled over a laptop furiously playing a typing game he was obsessed with at the time. Didn't he know he had three minutes before he had to take the stage? Didn't he know he was about to sing in front of thousands of screaming fans?

"Justin," I said sharply. "You have three minutes. Get off that stupid game!"

Not even bothering to look up, he remained glued to the computer, brushing me off as if I had just asked him to clean his room. "Wait. Just wait, Mom, I'm almost done. I'm about to beat my high score!"

I couldn't believe my ears. He wasn't the least bit concerned that time was ticking, that the pressure was on. That this was his moment.

"Justin," I snapped. "Get off the computer!"

"Hang on, Mom, just hang on. Let me finish this."

And just in the nick of time, less than a minute before he was due onstage and only seconds away from me grabbing the computer away from him, Justin slammed the lid shut. Looking at me with a huge grin, he jumped out of his seat and said, "Done!" He grabbed a nearby microphone and made a mad dash toward the stage. I heard Justin shout out without missing a beat, "How's it going, New York?" to the sound of a shrieking crowd.

Even as the pressure grew, he remained a typical teenager. I'll never forget what happened after one of his shows early on. We rushed out of the arena, having only thirty short minutes to make it to Justin's next radio appearance. Security officers surrounded us as we had to politely battle our way through the few hundred girls who were waiting outside for Justin. Our car seemed like it was a mile away, and I felt stuck in the midst of screaming teenagers and multiple pairs of outstretched arms that tried to reach out for Justin. Someone finally threw open the car door, and we hurried inside. I slammed the door shut and breathed a sigh of relief.

Driving off wasn't going to be easy. The girls wouldn't let us through. More security officers showed up to clear a path so we could drive out of the parking lot without running someone over.

The crowd was going crazy. The driver slowly inched his way through the screaming crowd onto the side street as girls pounded on the window. They chanted Justin's name and shrieked, "I love you, Justin!" The noise was deafening. The girls slammed on the car so hard, it felt like twenty-pound barbells were dropping out of the sky like rain. The car rocked back and forth from the mayhem.

I took in the moment, amused and shocked by the madness. *How the heck did we get here?* I wondered. *How did this happen?* Justin, however, didn't seem to notice the chaos. He simply picked up his cell phone and dialed his grandmother to say hello, chatting away as if he didn't have a clue what was happening outside. "How are you, Grandma?" he asked. "How was your day?" He wasn't Justin Bieber, pop star. He was Justin, grandson.

Despite how his career has exploded, Justin has always remained determined not to forget his roots. And I've done the same.

sixteen

Though I have experienced pain, shame, fear, and abandonment, I have also experienced hope, promise, peace, and joy. I get overwhelmed just thinking about how God has lavished me with His love and His grace—even in spite of my past, my mistakes, and my unfaithfulness. I love the verse in Psalms that says, "The LORD is close to the brokenhearted; he rescues those whose spirits are crushed" (34:18 NLT). It's the story of my life. I wouldn't wish my pain away because it has deepened my faith.

As Justin's career took off, I continued my healing journey. Though I started to face my demons and my past, the whole process took a long time. My healing even continues today. I don't want you to think I've arrived at the final destination of being emotionally whole, but I am so much freer, full of life and peace in so many areas in my life.

When I began to seek healing—through meeting with counselors, therapists, and mentors; by reading self-help books; and with lots of

> I promise you, there is always hope. Even if it doesn't look that way.

Seeking healing if you're hurting is one of the best things you can do for yourself. Emotional health is just as important as physical health.

prayer—I had no idea how many layers of pain I would have to work through. And I never knew how hard it would be.

At times I thought I was going to break under the pressure. I would remind myself of the Bible verse that shares how God "will not crush the weakest reed or put out a flickering candle" (Isa. 42:3 NLT). It told me that God is patient. And that He understood how broken I was and would be gentle with me. God wouldn't expect me to get it together immediately.

I think a big reason my healing took so long is because of the core lies I had believed since I was a little girl. The lies were formed by circumstances, people in my life, and even myself. It's taken me years to not only identify them but also replace them with truth. That was tough. I had to not only know something was true in my head but also believe it in my heart. Those are two different things. I had to grasp and embrace the truths (many of which are found in the Bible) and combat the lies with those truths.

When things are out of control and you can't change the situation you're in, trust that God is in control.

For instance, I used to believe the lie that I was unlovable; now I know the truth that I am loved (Rom. 8:39). I used to believe I was full of shame; now I know I am forgiven (Rom. 8:1). I used to believe I was worthless; now I know I am valuable (Ps. 139:14). I used to believe my life had no meaning; now I know the future is full of hope (Jer. 29:11). I used to feel rejected; now I know I am a daughter of God and my Father looks at me and is pleased (Zeph. 3:17). I used to believe I was a mistake; now I know I'm chosen (1 Pet. 2:9).

Whenever I felt depressed or anxious, I didn't let myself stay in that dark place. I fought my feelings with these truths (I still do when I need to). I focused on hope. I focused on the future. I focused on good things. The truth really does set you free.

My healing from the sexual abuse I'd suffered over the years was pretty complicated. I had to deal with the actual acts that happened as well as the aftermath. The abuse had created in me shame, anxiety, and fear. It had also messed up my view of love and sex. I believe so much of my brokenness came from the fact that I didn't value or respect my sexuality.

After I lost my virginity, having sex never felt wrong; it was just something I did. Something I was expected to do. But when I was twenty-one, I started feeling like I needed to address that part of my life.

As a Christian, I knew sex was supposed to be reserved for marriage. But a few years after I gave my life to God, I was still struggling in that area. At that time a youth pastor invited me to a True Love Waits conference. The timing was perfect.

As I listened to the message, my stomach was in knots. The speaker talked about his broken sexual past and how he reclaimed that part of his life. I wanted the same thing.

After the service, I signed a pledge—with my friend Kevin signing as a witness—not to have sex before I was married. My hand shook as I penned my name. It was time to heal the part of me that was broken. And to take seriously what I had once thought was no big deal.

I've kept my pledge. Yes, it's really hard. The temptation has been great at times. But I made a vow to God, something I don't take lightly. It may seem prudish or old-fashioned in this day and age, but I've committed to honoring God by saving myself for marriage. I have no intention of breaking that promise. (And yes, at the time of this writing, I'm still single.)

———

Forgiveness was also a big part of my healing process. It wasn't just others I had to forgive, though. I had to learn how to forgive myself. When I recently read the diary I had written during my teen years, it broke my heart. Drinking and smoking this much on that night. Getting wasted at a family get-together. Calling my mom every name in the book.

> Forgiveness is letting go of the right to get even.

I am a different person than I was when I wrote those things. I felt ashamed of how I acted and the things I did. At first, I wanted to throw away the diary. Maybe even burn it.

But I remembered the words, *Those who are hardest to love need it the most.* I love that statement. I say it all the time to remind myself to handle certain people with care. I say it to my parents. I say it to my friends. I say it to Justin. But I had to learn how to say it to myself. Sure, I loved myself, but I didn't love, let alone like very much, the hardened and rebellious teenager I used to be.

> *Unforgiveness is like drinking poison and waiting for the other person to die.*

I eventually learned how to forgive myself and stop hating the younger me for making stupid decisions and foolish choices. I can't love others if I don't love myself, so I'm learning how to love myself better.

I wasn't the only person I needed to forgive—there was my dad, my mom, my abusers, Jeremy. Sometimes the list felt so long. I started realizing that forgiveness is not a one-shot deal. Simply saying "I forgive you" doesn't take away the pain, the hurt, or the injustice that was done. I had to live from a place of forgiving all the time. Sometimes daily, sometimes even hourly. It wasn't easy and many times I had to ask God for help. And hey, if He forgave me for all the bad things I did, surely I could forgive others.

I realized if I didn't forgive others, I'd be the one ultimately hurt. I would become a bitter person, even wanting revenge of some kind. One definition of forgiving is letting go

> *"Take the first step in faith. You don't have to see the whole staircase, just take the first step."*
>
> —Martin Luther King, Jr.

of your right to get even. It doesn't mean the injustice was okay. While I didn't have a choice in how I was hurt or broken, I had a choice to forgive. I had a choice to let the pain define me or to heal from its wounds. I made the choice to heal. I made the choice to move on. I made the choice to live. To *really* live. It has not been easy, but it has been worth it.

I'm excited to see what's in store. This certainly isn't the end of my story. It's only the beginning.

There's more to me than just being Justin Bieber's mom. For the last eighteen years, I have dedicated my heart and soul to raising my son the best way I know how. Writing this book not only has been healing but is the first step into a new chapter of my life. I'm launching into my own destiny, which means figuring out more about my purpose and my mission in life.

The amazing platform God has given Justin has opened doors for me to share my story. When I was doing research for this book, I had the opportunity to visit the Bethesda Centre and talk to the girls there.

Though much of the building had been renovated and the rooms were rearranged, I felt a rush of memories. I could imagine myself as a scared teenager, trying to sort through a million questions and keep calm while battling a flurry of of emotions. Eighteen years later, and I still felt the anxiety of being pregnant. I felt the worry. The wonder. The pain.

As some of the staff showed me around the place, we stopped at a classroom where six girls who were either pregnant or new teen moms sat around a table. I smiled at their sweet faces. They looked so young and some of them so tired. I knew exactly what they must have been feeling in that moment—whether they were scared of the pain of giving birth, exhausted from lack of sleep from taking care of a new baby, or wondering what would happen to them after they left Bethesda and were on their own.

The girls talked loudly and giggled nonstop, bombarding me with all kinds of questions about (who else?) Justin, like if he still had a girlfriend and what it's like being the mom of a famous pop star. It wasn't long, however, before they started talking about serious things.

One feisty girl who had gotten unusually quiet lowered her head and timidly lifted up her hand. I nodded toward her and she began to speak, her eyes full of tears.

"I feel like I have nothing to offer my baby," she sobbed. My heart broke as she continued to cry. I walked over to her and gave her a hug, holding her close for a few minutes. I imagine very few teen moms don't feel the same way.

I encouraged this precious girl. "I didn't feel like I had anything to offer either," I admitted. "I was young when I had Justin, and I had been through a lot of sexual abuse and hard stuff. It's part of the reason I'm here. I know how tough it is. I know exactly how you feel."

I looked her in the eye and continued. "What do you have to offer? Love. Love is so powerful. And you have yourself to offer. It's more than enough. If you take care of yourself, your life, and your heart, you can offer so much! Look at the kids who are born in third world countries. Their parents don't have much to give them except themselves and their hearts. And those children are some of the happiest in the world! Trust me, you have plenty to offer your baby."

I felt humbled by this girl's honesty and honored that I could share with her my experiences, my insecurities, and my doubts and show her through my life that she could be a good mother to her baby, no matter how old she was.

I will always have a special place in my heart for teen mothers. But it's not just teen moms who struggle or need to find hope. Whether you're a teen single mom or a victim of abuse . . . whether you're struggling in school or being bullied . . . whether you're in a dysfunctional family or the product of a broken home . . . whether you're depressed or struggle with anxiety . . . whether you live in fear or hide in shame . . . whether you've been abandoned, rejected, or ignored—there is hope.

It doesn't matter where you find yourself today—how broken, hurting, wounded, or ashamed you are. If God can help me find my way up, I promise, He can do the same for you.

Acknowledgments

To my son, Justin, my heart: I'm proud of you beyond words. You've brought so much joy into my life, and I've always known you were created for greatness. I'm grateful for you standing with me through this writing process. I know I haven't been able to travel with you as much lately. Know that I've missed you. (PS: I just had a burst of love for you.)

To my parents: Mom, you are and always have been a good mother. I'll always be grateful for your sacrifices for our family, from staying up nights when we were sick, to always being around, to cooking and cleaning every day and doing whatever it took to provide for our needs. Thank you, Mom. I love you. Bruce, thank you for being an amazing husband to my mom and loving her like you do. I know I wasn't always the easiest daughter, but you were always a good and faithful dad. (I never did grow up to be that boxer, but I did write a book!) You both are unbelievable grandparents.

To my siblings: Candie, I always looked up to you. You were a great big sister. Thanks for always listening to me and giving me advice. Chris, thanks for being a protective older brother and always scaring the bullies away. Sorry for always getting you in trouble when we were younger. To the other Chris, thanks for letting us call you Chuck and for being sweet and always making me laugh. Sally, I can't wait to meet you in heaven.

To Jeremy: I'm eternally grateful to you not only for giving me the greatest gift of my life, Justin, but also for becoming the man and father you are today. Though our relationship was rocky, I wouldn't take any of it back or change any of it because God has turned it all around for good and continues to do so. My intentions are not to hurt you. With that said, this is my side of the story that could not be possible without you. I love you. There will always be a special place in my heart for you.

To Lesley, my publicist and my assistant/manager/advisor/ whatever-I-need-in-the-moment beast: You are amazing! Above all else, you are a really great friend. I treasure you.

To A. J., my co-writer, a wife, a mother to a baby girl, and an author: I honestly don't know how you do it. You work harder than any woman I know and somehow still manage to produce the gold. After countless hours together, I have gained a friend. We did it!

To Esther, my literary agent: Thank you for believing in me. You're the best at what you do.

To Dwight Baker and the team at Revell: Thank you for your hard work, your patience, your diligence, and your expertise. A special thanks to Jennifer and Twila for going the extra mile (specifically, 267 miles for Jen to drive to Canada).

To my abusers: I forgive you.

Discussion Questions

Chapter 1

1. I had a hard time feeling like I belonged in my family. Have you had any similar feelings? If so, why? Maybe your parents got divorced and you felt torn between the two, or you struggled to accept your new stepfamily.

2. Have you experienced parental abandonment? Maybe you never met your mom or dad, your parents are separated or divorced, or they work so much that you don't regularly see them. How do you deal with your feelings of rejection? Have you talked to someone about how you feel, like a friend or guidance counselor?

Chapter 2

1. Sometimes it may be confusing to understand what sexual abuse is. Children can misinterpret inappropriate touching as someone simply being overly friendly. How do you define

189

sexual abuse? Go back to page 20 and read the definition again. Does this change how you define it?

2. Has anyone ever touched you in an inappropriate way? Or has someone made you do something sexually that you didn't like and that made you feel uncomfortable? If so, did you tell a trusted friend or adult? If not, what kept you from telling? Were you scared? Ashamed?

3. Do you have a distant relationship with one of your parents? Maybe your mom or dad divorced when you were young or you just can't seem to talk to them. Do you miss feeling close to them? Are you angry about how things are?

4. Most victims of sexual abuse struggle with low self-esteem and shame because they keep quiet about their abuse. Why is it important to use your voice and speak up against sexual abuse?

Chapter 3

1. What is the difference between feeling sad and being depressed? Have you ever struggled with depression or known someone who has? Why is getting help such a big deal?

2. How would you describe your relationship with your parents? What do they do that frustrates you? Have you ever reacted badly (yelled, disobeyed, called them names) and regretted it later? What would have been a better way of reacting? What will you do differently next time?

3. Have you ever felt rejected by your peers? Was there a specific instance that made you feel this way (like when my group of friends told me they didn't want me to be their friend anymore)? How did it make you feel?

What lies did you believe as a result (for example, "There's something wrong with me" or "I'm not good enough")?

What are the truths you need to believe instead (for example, "There is nothing wrong with me" or "I am good enough")?

4. Have you ever acted out in rebellion (stealing, drinking, doing drugs, being disrespectful toward your parents or other authority figures) because you struggled with hurt or depression and didn't know what to do about it? Did anyone try to help you? Did you seek help?

5. How would it make you feel if you told someone you were sexually abused and they didn't believe you? Has this happened to you? Or has anyone ever shared with you how they were sexually abused? How did you respond?

Chapter 4

1. Are you or is anyone you know in a physically, psychologically, or emotionally abusive relationship? Does your boyfriend tear you down instead of build you up? What will it take for you to call it quits? How can you encourage a friend in that situation to leave?

2. People who have been abused are often attracted to those who are abusive because it's familiar. It's important to choose friends who treat us with respect and with love. No one deserves to be treated poorly. How can you avoid having friendships or romantic relationships with people who are psychologically, emotionally, or even physically abusive?

3. Have you ever gotten drunk or high and done something you regretted later? If so, did you feel so bad that you vowed not

to do it again? Did you keep your promise? (If you haven't done this, has someone you know?)

Chapter 5

1. What are some common warning signs that a person might commit suicide (see page 65)? What can you do to help a friend you fear might kill herself or himself?

2. Have you ever tried to help a friend who was really depressed or hurting? Did that friend accept your help? If not, what did you do?

3. How does faith fit into your life? Somewhat? A lot? Not at all? Why or why not?

4. Have you ever made a positive change in your life but did not get the support of your friends? How did that make you feel? Did you break ties with them?

Chapter 6

1. Have you ever felt pressured to drink, do drugs, or have sex? Did you go through with it even if you didn't want to? What were some of the consequences of your actions? What could have stopped you from falling under the pressure?

2. Do you think sex is a big deal? Why or why not? Besides pregnancy, what are some of the consequences of premarital sex (see pages 79–80 for more facts)? How would your life change if you were diagnosed with an STD? What would motivate you to wait until you got married to have sex?

3. Do you think it's old-fashioned or weird to be a virgin? Why or why not?

4. How would your life change if you got pregnant (or fathered a child) as an unwed teenager? What would be different?

Chapter 7

1. Do you know anyone who is a teen parent? What do you think is the hardest thing about having a baby so young? If you are already a teen parent, what has been the most difficult challenge?

2. If you got pregnant or became a teen dad today, how would you react? Who would you tell? Would your parents be supportive? Do you think you are ready to be a parent? Would you regret having sex before marriage?

3. Why do you think God designed sex to take place in the confines of marriage? What do you think are some of the benefits of waiting?

4. If you are in a desperate situation right now, do you believe God can help you get through it? Do you believe He forgives us no matter what we've done or how big our past mistakes are?

Chapter 8

1. Do you think it's healthy to break up and get back together with your boyfriend or girlfriend many times? Why is it so hard for some people (maybe even you) to stay away from a toxic relationship?

2. I believe the best kind of romantic relationship is based on similar values and principles—a shared faith—and happens when both parties are emotionally healthy. It's especially important for both people to understand the other is not

meant to "save" them or be their everything. Do you agree or disagree? And why?

Chapter 9

1. What are some of the responsibilities a young teen mom has in caring for her baby? Does it seem like a lot to handle on your own? What are some of the things you would have to give up?

2. Many teens quit high school, for lots of different reasons. Some never graduate because they think an education is pointless. What are some reasons to stay in school?

3. How are you doing in school? Do you enjoy any of your classes? Do you study hard and do your best? Why or why not?

4. Has anyone done anything kind for you for no other reason than that they wanted to (and didn't ask for anything back in return)? How did it make you feel? Have you returned that kindness to anyone else?

Chapter 10

1. Why is it important for parents to discipline their kids? How do your parents react if you get in trouble? Do you think they are too strict, too easy, or fair in disciplining you?

2. Have you ever felt disrespected by an authority figure (like a parent or teacher)? How can you honor or respect an adult even when you feel you are being treated unfairly (for example, by listening and not talking back)?

3. What are some of your natural talents? Do you have opportunities to use and grow your gifts? If not, how can you spend more time working on the skills that come naturally to you and that you enjoy doing?

Chapter 11

1. Are you surrounded by people (friends, family) who believe in you? If so, how does that encourage you? If not, how does not having a network of support affect you? Is there a person or group (like a school club, youth group, or volunteer group) that you can connect with to feel more supported?

2. What are some fun things you have done with your parents? Do you wish you could spend more time with them doing things you all enjoy? If so, how can you initiate some fun activities to do together?

3. Have you suffered a traumatic experience that you still feel the effects of even though it happened a long time ago? Have you told anyone about it? If not, who can you talk to and get help?

Chapter 12

1. When was the last time you stepped out of your comfort zone and did something positive even though you were scared (like try out for the school play, enter a race, or start a new club at school)? What can motivate you to take a healthy risk and try something new?

2. Is there something that you enjoy doing and want to excel at, like a sport, a musical instrument, or a subject in school? If so, what can you do to make sure you are doing your best?

3. No one can come in first place all the time. When was the last time you experienced a loss (whether the soccer championship or a contest)? How did you handle it? What are some healthy ways to react to a loss? Did someone encourage you even though you didn't take the top spot?

4. All of us find ourselves gossiping about others from time to time. How can you prevent yourself from talking badly about others or spreading rumors? How do you handle negative comments or gossip from others?

Chapter 13

1. Goals and dreams are something you want to do, have, or be. Do you have any that you'd like to pursue? What are some of them?

2. Do you feel your parents support you in your dreams or goals? If not, how can they do a better job?

3. Have you ever had a difficult decision to make? Maybe deciding whether or not to break up with your boyfriend, or to stop hanging around friends who may be a bad influence, or handling a peer pressure situation. Who do you go to for advice or support?

Chapter 14

1. Have you ever traveled to a new place, different from your hometown? What was the experience like for you? What did you enjoy about it?

2. How do you define "values"? Are they important to you? Do you use them to help shape your decisions? Why or why not?

3. Have you ever had to say goodbye to something or someone? Maybe you moved to a different city or your best friend transferred to a new school. Was it difficult to deal with? If so, how did you manage your emotions?

Chapter 15

1. Have you ever had to make a major life change, like attending a new school or dealing with your parents' divorce? Did you have friends or family to rely on during this difficult time? How can you be a friend to someone who is going through a major life change?

2. I am dependent on my faith for direction and peace in my heart. Who or what do you turn to when you feel lonely or unsure or need help?

Chapter 16

1. When you go through a traumatic or hurtful event, the pain of the experience will stay with you until you deal with it. It doesn't just go away. It can affect your emotions and even make you physically sick. Have you ever kept something inside and not dealt with it? What are some ways to ask for or get help?

2. One of the ways I found healing was in changing the "core lies" I believed about myself, like how worthless I thought I was. Do you believe similar lies? Is it so hard for you to believe the truth that you are valuable and worth it? Why or why not?

Take a few minutes to read about how God sees you as "fearfully and wonderfully made" in Psalm 139 in the Bible.

3. Forgiving others (and myself) was another necessary part of my healing journey (see page 182). Are there people in your life who have hurt you and who you need to forgive?

I want to thank you for taking the time to think about your life and your experiences when you answered these questions. I'm sure some were hard to answer. It takes a lot of courage to be honest with yourself and maybe even admit some things you'd never told anyone before. I'm proud of you for doing that!

You may be struggling with issues like abuse, depression, or suicidal thoughts. I want to encourage you to find healing. No matter how bad things are, what you may have done, or what was done to you, you can have a better life. Your heart can be whole. You can feel good about yourself. If you need help, reach out to an adult you can trust, or contact one of the organizations listed in the Resources section.

I went through many things that broke my heart, but I've learned that God always has a bigger plan. You can't change what has happened in the past, but you can take the first step toward a greater future. Trust God. He loves you more than you know. If He can bring me up from a place of pain, rejection, and hurt, I know He can do the same for you.

Notes

1. American Academy of Child & Adolescent Psychology, "Child Sexual Abuse," March 2011, http://aacap.org/page.ww?name=Child+Sexual+Abuse&section =Facts+for+Families; American Psychological Association, "Child Sexual Abuse: What Parents Should Know," 2013, http://www.apa.org/pi/families/resources /child-sexual-abuse.aspx.

2. American Psychological Association, "Child Sexual Abuse: What Parents Should Know."

3. Stephanie Faris, "Depression Statistics," Healthline, March 28, 2012, http:// www.healthline.com/health/depression/statistics.

4. The Confidence Coalition, "The Cause," 2010, http://www.confidencecoali tion.org/teens-thecause.

5. "Cyber Bullying: Statistics and Tips," i-SAFE, 2004, http://www.isafe.org/ outreach/media/media_cyber_bullying.

6. "National Survey of American Attitudes on Substance Abuse XVII: Teens," the National Center on Addiction and Substance Abuse at Columbia University, August 2012, http://www.casacolumbia.org/upload/2012/20120822teensurvey.pdf.

7. Megan Foreman and Martha Saenz, "Preventing Teen Suicide," National Conference of State Legislators, *LegisBrief* 18, no. 25 (April–May 2010), http:// www.ncsl.org/issues-research/health/preventing-teen-suicide.aspx.

8. "Facts and Figures: National Statistics," American Foundation for Suicide Prevention, 2013, http://www.afsp.org/index.cfm?fuseaction=home.viewpage &page_id=050fea9f-b064-4092-b1135c3a70de1fda.

9. Amy L. Sutton, ed., *Sexually Transmitted Diseases Sourcebook* (Detroit: Om- nigraphics, 2006), quoted at http://facts.randomhistory.com/2009/09/07_std.html.

10. Centers for Disease Control, "CDC Fact Sheet: STD Trends in the United States," December 2012, http://www.cdc.gov/std/stats11/trends-2011.pdf.

11. Jennifer Shoquist, MD, and Diane Stafford, *The Encyclopedia of Sexually Transmitted Diseases* (New York: Facts on File, 2004), quoted at http://facts. randomhistory.com/2009/09/07_std.html.

12. Laura Egendorf, ed., *Sexually Transmitted Diseases* (New York: Thompson Gale, 2007), quoted at http://facts.randomhistory.com/2009/09/07_std.html.

13. The National Campaign to Prevent Teen and Unplanned Pregnancies, "With One Voice 2012," August 2012, http://www.thenationalcampaign.org/resources/pdf/pubs/WOV_2012.pdf.

14. "High School Dropout Statistics," Statistic Brain, October 2012, http://www.statisticbrain.com/high-school-dropout-statistics.

15. Ibid.

16. Ibid.

17. Wendy Schwartz, "New Information on Youth Who Drop Out: Why They Leave and What Happens to Them," KidSource Online, April 20, 2000, http://www.kidsource.com/kidsource/content4/youth.drop.out.html.

18. "School Dropouts," Report to the Honorable Jim Gibbons, House of Representatives, United States General Accounting Office, February 2002, http://www.gao.gov/new.items/d02240.pdf, 4.

19. National Institute of Mental Health, http://www.nimh.nih.gov/statistics/1ANYANX_child.shtml.

Resources

Sexual Abuse/Rape:

National Sexual Assault Hotline (24/7): 1-800-656-HOPE (4673)

Childhelp National Child Abuse Hotline (24/7): 1-800-4-A-CHILD (422-4453)

Depression/Suicide:

National Suicide Hotline (24/7): 1-800-SUICIDE

National Suicide Prevention Hotline (24/7): 1-800-273-TALK (8255)

American Foundation for Suicide Prevention: http://www.afsp.org

The Society for the Prevention of Teen Suicide: http://www.sptsusa.org

Substance Abuse:

The National Alcohol and Substance Abuse Information Center (24/7): 1-800-784-6776

Alcohol Abuse:

National Council on Alcoholism and Drug Dependence (24/7): 1-800-622-2255

Alateen: http://www.al-anon.alateen.org/for-alateen

Domestic Violence:

National Domestic Violence Hotline: 1-800-799-SAFE (7233)

Pattie Mallette, known to most of the world as Justin Bieber's mom, is more than just the mother of a world-renowned pop sensation. She grew up in Stratford, Ontario, overcoming unimaginable obstacles in the face of abuse, poverty, and an unexpected teen pregnancy. She now uses her voice to inspire others as a bestselling author, producer, and influential speaker.

In 2012, Pattie published her memoir, *Nowhere but Up*, which became a *New York Times* bestseller within the first week of its release. She worked as an executive producer on *Crescendo*, a short film that received 11 international film festival honors prior to its US premier in February 2013. Proceeds from *Crescendo* are being used to support crisis pregnancy centers worldwide, a passion of Pattie's that grew from her own experience. As a single parent at 18, Pattie was personally assisted by such a center, which enabled her, despite her difficult circumstances, to be the best mother possible to her son, Justin.

Continuing to follow her desire to help others give voice to their own stories, Pattie became an executive producer of the feature film *Renee*, starring Kat Dennings (*2 Broke Girls*). Set to release in winter 2013, the film is inspired by the true story behind the global movement To Write Love on Her Arms.

Pattie recently launched her foundation called Round 2, which seeks to offer a second chance to those who have been knocked down by providing assistance and resources to those in distress.

Across all platforms, Pattie's authenticity and candidness are magnetic to adolescents and adults alike as she fearlessly brings to light her own wounds and addresses sensitive issues with wisdom and insight.

A. J. Gregory is the author of *Messy Faith* and *Silent Savior*, which chronicles finding faith in the middle of unavoidable and sometimes harsh realities. She also partners with celebrities, military leaders, life coaches, pastors, physicians, and professors to help them write their own stories. An accomplished writer, A. J. has collaborated with fascinating high-profile figures on over twenty-five books.